Jean-Luc Godard's *Pierrot le fou*

Jean-Luc Godard's *Pierrot le fou,* made at the height of the French New Wave, remains a milestone in French cinema. More accessible than his later films, it represents the diverse facets of Godard's concerns and themes: a bittersweet analysis of male-female relations, an interrogation of the image, personal and international politics, and the existential dilemmas of consumer society. This volume brings together essays by five prominent scholars of French film. They approach *Pierrot le fou* from the perspectives of image and wordplay, aesthetics and politics, history, and high and popular culture, offering thought-provoking insights into the film while demonstrating its relevance for a new generation of students of film. Also included are a selection of reviews of the film, as well as a complete filmography of Godard's work.

David Wills is chair of the Department of Languages, Literatures, and Cultures at the University at Albany, SUNY. A scholar of French literature and film, he is the author of *Prosthesis,* co-author of *Screen/Play: Derrida and Film Theory,* and co-editor of *Deconstruction and the Visual Arts: Art, Media and Architecture.*

Jean-Luc Godard's *Pierrot le fou*

Jean-Luc Godard

THE CAMBRIDGE UNIVERSITY PRESS FILM HANDBOOKS SERIES

General Editor

Andrew Horton, *University of Oklahoma*

Each CAMBRIDGE FILM HANDBOOK is intended to focus on a single film from a variety of theoretical, critical, and contextual perspectives. This "prism" approach is designed to give students and general readers valuable background and insight into the cinematic, artistic, cultural, and sociopolitical importance of individual films by including chapters by leading film scholars and critics. Furthermore, these handbooks by their very nature are meant to help the reader better grasp the nature of the critical and theoretical discourse on cinema as an art form, as a visual medium, and as a cultural product. Filmographies and select bibliographies are included to help the reader go further on his or her own exploration of the film under consideration.

Jean-Luc Godard's
Pierrot le fou

Edited by
DAVID WILLS

CAMBRIDGE UNIVERSITY PRESS
Cambridge, New York, Melbourne, Madrid, Cape Town,
Singapore, São Paulo, Delhi, Mexico City

Cambridge University Press
The Edinburgh Building, Cambridge CB2 8RU, UK

Published in the United States of America by Cambridge University Press, New York

www.cambridge.org
Information on this title: www.cambridge.org/9780521574891

First published 2000

A catalogue record for this publication is available from the British Library

Library of Congress Cataloguing in Publication Data

Jean-Luc Godard's Pierrot le fou / edited by David Wills.
    p.   cm. – (Cambridge film handbooks)
    Filmography: p.
    Includes bibliographical references
    ISBN 0-521-57375-0 (hardcover)
    1. Pierrot le fou (Motion picture) I. Wills, David, 1953–
II. Series. Cambridge film handbooks series.
PN1997.P482 J43   2000
791.43'72 – dc21   99-043660

ISBN 978-0-521-57375-7 Hardback
ISBN 978-0-521-57489-1 Paperback

Contents

Acknowledgments

I wish to thank, in the first place, Andy Horton, the series editor, for inviting me to edit this volume and for encouraging its progress across a number of continents; and, in the second place, the contributors for their enthusiasm and cooperation.

I am most grateful to David Laatsch, a graduate assistant in the French program at Louisiana State University, for his assiduous bibliographical research and preparation of reprinted reviews of *Pierrot le fou* that appear at the end of the volume. His draft translations of those and other materials, acknowledged in the text, were invaluable in speeding up the editing process.

Film stills from *Breathless, Pierrot le fou,* and Abel Gance's *Napoleon* are provided courtesy of the Museum of Modern Art Film Stills Archive. I am most grateful to Mary Corliss and Terry Geesken for their assistance in providing these illustrations. Thanks are also due to David Sterritt and Jonathan Rosenbaum for assistance with the filmography.

Note on References and Abbreviations

Two important texts are referred to in both French and English editions.

The French script of the film appears in the journal *L'Avant-Scène Cinéma* 171–2 (1976). It is translated as *Pierrot le fou: A Film by Jean-Luc Godard,* trans. Peter Whitehead (London: Lorrimer Publishing/New York: Simon & Schuster, 1969). The translation also contains extracts from the *Cahiers du cinéma* interview "Let's Talk About Pierrot" (N&M, 215–34; B, 263–80 [see next paragraph for these references]). Note that various discrepancies exist between the spoken French dialogue and the *Avant-Scène* transcription, and between the Whitehead translation and the subtitles to the English version of the film. Throughout this volume the French and English published transcripts are referred to in the text as, respectively, *A-S* and W, followed by a page number. When the Whitehead translation is not followed, indicated by "cf. W," the translation is by the respective contributor.

A collection of interviews with and writings by Godard is published in French as Alain Bergala (ed.), *Jean-Luc Godard par Jean-Luc Godard* (Paris: Cahiers du Cinéma-Éditions de l'Étoile, 1985). An earlier edition (Paris: Pierre Belfond, 1968), covering Godard's work up to and including *Deux ou trois choses que je sais d'elle/Two or Three Things I Know About Her* (1966), exists in English translation as Jean Narboni and Tom Milne (eds.), *Godard on Godard* (New York: Da Capo, 1986). (This is a reprint of the 1972 Viking edition. The new edition lists Tom Milne as editor and translator.)

Throughout this volume the French and English editions are referred to in the text as, respectively, B and N&M, followed by a page number. Whenever the French edition (B) only is indicated, the reference is to matter not included in the translation. In such cases the translation is by the respective contributor.

Contributors

Tom Conley is Professor of French at Harvard University. His books include *Film Hieroglyphs, The Graphic Unconscious in Early Modern French Literature* (also published in French), and *The Self-Made Map: Cartographical Literature in Early Modern France.* He has translated Deleuze's *The Fold* and Michel de Certeau's *The Deluge, the Plague: Paolo Uccello,* and *The Capture of Speech and Culture in the Plural,* and Christian Jacob's *The Sovereign Map.* He is completing a study on space, event, and violence in critical writing.

Richard Dienst is Associate Professor in the department of English at Rutgers University and author of a groundbreaking work on television that uses Godard as an essential reference, *Still Life in Real Time: Theory After Television.* He has also published articles and essays in the areas of cultural studies, media politics, and the imaginary dimensions of economics, and has two volumes forthcoming: *The Shape of the World* (with Henry Schwarz), and, on indebtedness and the global economy, *Who Owes the World?*

Jill Forbes is Professor of French at Queen Mary and Westfield, University of London, a film critic, and former governor of the British Film Institute. A specialist in French cultural studies and postwar French culture and society, she has published important works in French cinema including a study of the Marcel Carné classic, *Les Enfants du paradis,* and *The Cinema in France: After the New Wave.* Other published works include *Contemporary France* and *French Cultural Studies: An Introduction* (co-editor Michael Kelly).

Jean-Louis Leutrat is Professor of Film Studies and President of the Université de Paris III – Sorbonne Nouvelle. He has published books on French writer Julien Gracq as well as in various areas of film studies, among them the western, Nosferatu, the fantastic, and Godard. Titles include *L'Alliance brisée: le Western des années 1920, Le Cinéma en perspective: une Histoire, Vie des fantômes, L'Année dernière à Marienbad, Jean-Luc Godard* (with Suzanne Liandrat-Guigues), and *L'Autre visible* (with Francis Jacques).

Alan Williams is Professor of French, Comparative Literature, and Cinema Studies at Rutgers University and the author of many essays on film, including work on Godard and sound, and *Max Ophuls and the Cinema of Desire*. His 1992 book, *Republic of Images: A History of French Filmmaking,* is the first general and comprehensive history of French film to appear in English. He is the editor of the forthcoming *Film and Nationalism* and is currently writing a history of American "studio system" filmmaking from 1915 to 1960.

David Wills is Professor of French and English and chair of the Department of Languages, Literatures, and Cultures at the University at Albany (SUNY). His publications include *Screen/Play: Derrida and Film Theory* (co-author Peter Brunette), *Writing Pynchon* (co-author Alec McHoul), *Deconstruction and the Visual Arts* (co-editor Peter Brunette), and *Prosthesis,* which he has also translated into French. He is translator of Derrida's *Gift of Death* and *Right of Inspection,* and is currently writing a book on jazz.

DAVID WILLS

Introduction

OUI, BIEN SÛR ... OUI, BIEN SÛR

A complicated story – all mixed up

There are good reasons for maintaining that, during the five or so years before *Pierrot le fou* was released in 1965, Western cinema had for the second or third, and perhaps last time in its history, been reinvented. Within that perspective, the first reinvention would have been the innovative theoretical approaches to film-making developed by Eisenstein in the 1920s; the second, Italian neo-realism; and the third, the French New Wave. Jean-Luc Godard was foremost among the group of cinéastes for whom a journalist coined the term *New Wave,* and his 1960 feature *A bout de souffle/Breathless* was considered a pioneering moment in breaking with certain of the restricting practices of the cinema of the time while also renewing enthusiastically the possibilities that the medium seemed to offer. The New Wave directors, often friends and associates but never a coherent movement, were a group of mostly young practitioners like Godard that included François Truffaut, Éric Rohmer, Jacques Rivette, Claude Chabrol, Alain Resnais, and Agnès Varda.

By the time of *Pierrot le fou,* Godard's films had variously been acclaimed at festivals (*Vivre sa vie/My Life to Live,* 1962) or forbidden release by the French government (*Le Petit soldat,* 1960/63), attracted the collaboration of stars like Brigitte Bardot (*Le Mépris/Contempt,* 1963) or flopped at the box office (*Les Carabiniers,* 1963). The director was nothing if not notorious, and to

I

this day, as he continues to make films that more than occasionally intrigue and fascinate a jaded audience of critics and spectators, he remains widely respected as the enfant terrible of cinema.[1]

Godard, born in Paris in 1930 into a Swiss family, initially intended to write fiction, but his interest in cinema led him to contribute to a series of film journals, including the *Cahiers du cinéma* founded by André Bazin, and to frequent the film clubs and *Cinémathèque* where he met many of the filmmakers who would become his fellow travelers. Eventually, with the help and financial support of that same network, he began to make his own films. But there was much to distinguish him from other New Wave directors, not the least reasons being his improvisational approach to script and to shooting, and his editing practice, in particular his use of what came to be known as the jump cut, which unsettles the viewer by giving the impression of jumping to another scene before the preceding one has played out as we would expect it to from our training as spectators of classic film and of theater.[2] Viewers of *A bout de souffle* who have been weaned on MTV will of course be less surprised by the jump cut than was the audience of 1959, but conversely, we might argue that it is thanks to the innovations of Godard that a film like *Natural Born Killers* (Oliver Stone, 1994) can be conceived of. Similarly – for the idea of the jump cut allows for sequences to be inordinately lengthened as well as shortened – we can see the timing and direction of Quentin Tarantino, for example the remarkable opening diner sequence of *Reservoir Dogs* (1992) or the extended bantering scenes in *Pulp Fiction* (1994), as conscious homages to the possibilities created for cinema by the New Wave, possibilities that much contemporary film, in its desire for the perfect illusion, leaves unexploited. For in the final analysis, Godard resolved to make his films about cinema, or at least about the image. He was from a generation that was enamored of films, and indiscriminately devoured them, a group of filmmakers whose literacy in terms of cinema was at the time unsurpassed. For him, the only subject of the films of that period was "cinema itself,"[3] and indeed the same might be said of all his work. It constitutes nothing so much as an interrogation of the possibilities of the image, of the role of the image in our culture, and as such is unique in the history of the cinema, and of the culture and the century that has adopted the moving image as one of its most popular art forms.

In accounts of Godard's work, the period of *Pierrot le fou* is also referred to as the "Anna Karina years," and the director's personal and professional collaboration with the Danish actress playing the film's female protagonist, whom he married in 1961, structures the work of 1960 to 1967.[4] These were also the years of Godard's greatest commercial success, and indeed critical reaction to *Pierrot* was, in France at least, the most positive the director was ever to receive. He had bought the rights to Lionel White's novel *Obsession* in 1963, and intended to make the film with well-known actress and singer Sylvie Vartan, and then with Richard Burton. Finally Godard was able to pair Anna Karina, working with him for the sixth time, with the antihero par excellence of *A bout de souffle,* Jean-Paul Belmondo, in order to tell "the story of the last romantic couple" (N&M, 216; B, 263). But two days before shooting was to begin, he had nothing to go on apart from the book and the idea for a certain number of sets. Lines were therefore rehearsed on the set, or improvised, and the film was shot, in Godard's words, "like in the days of Mack Sennett . . . the whole last part was invented on the spot, unlike the beginning, which was planned. It is a kind of happening, but one that was controlled" (N&M, 218; B, 265). Filming took place over two months, July and August 1965, on the Côte d'Azur, on the island of Porquerolles, and finally in Paris, in reverse order to the events of the film. It was shot in cinemascope by Raoul Coutard, who had worked on all of Godard's feature films up to that point, who would remain with him throughout the Karina years and return again in the 1980s. Jean-Pierre Léaud, Truffaut's favorite actor, was a director's assistant (and a film spectator in one scene), and the producer Georges de Beauregard, another faithful collaborator, financed the film.

Pierrot follows the adventures of Ferdinand (Belmondo), fleeing a stultifying bourgeois existence, and Marianne (Karina), his free-spirited lover, in their escapades through the south of France en route to a romantic utopia they never find. The film begins, after a series of autonomous shots, with Ferdinand sitting in the bath reading to his daughter from a book about the artist Diego Velázquez. He is then seen dressing for a cocktail party where, as his wife reminds him, he should behave properly so as to impress potential employers because he has recently been fired from (or given up) his job in television. The baby-sitter, supposedly the niece of friends who arrive to accompany Ferdinand and his wife to the party, is Marianne.

The scenes at the party, filmed through different-colored filters, include parodies of advertisements for cars and women's beauty products, as well as the short appearance by Samuel Fuller and his definition of cinema as "emotion," which becomes the focus of much and varied discussion in the contributions that follow. The party shows up the sterility of Ferdinand's existence, leading to his precipitate departure and return home where he offers to drive Marianne back to her house. It is only once the couple is in the car that the spectator understands they have already been romantically involved. The scene ends with a short exchange resembling a series of vows: "I'll do anything you want," says Marianne; "Me too, Marianne," replies Ferdinand; "I'm putting my hand on your knee," "Me too, Marianne"; "I'm kissing you all over," "Me too, Marianne," although the characters continue to stare ahead out of the car windshield (A-S, 76–8; cf. W, 37). This, however, becomes the point of rupture in Ferdinand's life and the point of departure for what will amount to a permanent flight, from Paris, from family, from the law, from enemies, ending only with the death of both protagonists at the end of the film.

The next morning Pierrot (he keeps reminding her that his name is Ferdinand, but, as she replies, one can't say "mon ami Ferdinand" as in the song "Au clair de la lune, mon ami Pierrot") and Marianne wake up at what we take to be her apartment, but it is an apartment containing crates of guns as well as a dead body, and they are interrupted by her "uncle," whom they knock unconscious in the first of a series of slapstick scenes, before fleeing Paris for the countryside en route to the Riviera. The rest of the film is a

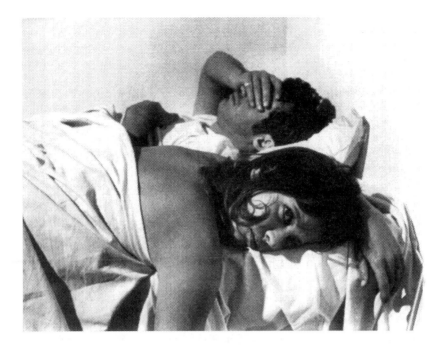

Marianne and Pierrot the next morning

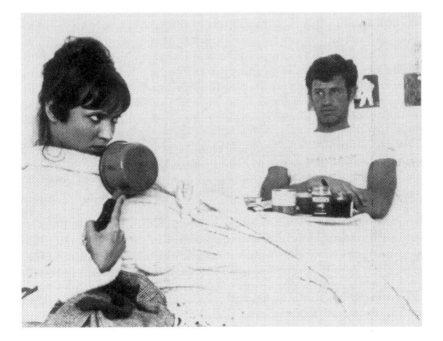

series of mostly unconnected episodes from that escapade with, on the one hand scenes of a tense and finally fractured relationship between Pierrot and Marianne, and on the other hand, a disconnected story of gunrunning for royalists in Yemen, and Marianne's supposed or actual infidelity with the person she has introduced as her brother. A number of these scenes are memorable for their cinematic or theatrical resourcefulness. There is the semi slapstick of a roadside garage sequence that reminds us of Godard's respect for early cinema as well as the fact that Pierrot is an obvious reference to the *commedia del arte* theatrical tradition (*A-S*, 80; W, 44–5). Another sequence, revealing Godard's increasingly vocal political sensibilities and the increasing importance of opposition to America's involvement in Vietnam, has Pierrot and Marianne performing a minimalist theatrical piece for some attentive Americans whom they proceed to rob (*A-S*, 92; W, 70–2). There are also musical numbers (*A-S*, 78, 93; W, 38–9, 73–4), a scene where Pierrot undergoes a wet-towel torture that was used by the French in Algeria (*A-S*, 96–7; W, 80–1), and a humorous sequence by comic Raymond Devos (*A-S*, 106; W, 100–1).

In the relationship with Pierrot, Marianne seems to be continually raising the stakes in terms of what she expects from him, and lowering them in terms of what promises she will keep. He never seems to know what he really wants and appears powerless to attain it, as if since the beginning he had been drifting and then drawn into Marianne's sphere of influence. But she is by no means a simple character. Indeed, it has been well pointed out that the female character in many of Godard's films, and in *Pierrot* in particular, is presented on the one hand as strong, almost masculine – wielding a gun or a pair of scissors, asking forthrightly for what she wants or expects – and on the other hand as an unattainable romantic ideal.[5] As if to demonstrate his frustration at being unable to pin her down, and on the pretext of her infidelity, Pierrot finally kills her, calls his wife in Paris but fails to get through, then paints his face blue and winds a whole arsenal of dynamite about his head before lighting the fuse. In what can be taken as his first and last decisive act, he tries to extinguish the fuse with

Marianne as violent otherness

his hand, but, unable to see it, dies in a flash of flame and smoke against the brilliant blue of the Mediterranean sea and sky.

THE END OF CINEMA?

It seems that the years 1967–8 would have marked an important break in Godard's filmmaking, even if that period had not also been contemporaneous with the upheaval in French social, cultural, and political life that took place in May 1968, when students and workers took to the streets en masse to demand that the country begin to chart a new, more open course. The events of that period have been discussed extensively, and Godard's part in them was not negligible, arguing for the closure of the Cannes festival, participating in the "Estates-General of Cinema" and in various "agit-prop" film productions.[6] But the increasingly political slant of Godard's cinema was already explicit in the films immediately following *Pierrot le fou,* and especially in *La Chinoise* (1967) and *Week-end* (1967). Godard ends his 1966 film *Deux ou trois choses que je sais d'elle/Two or Three Things I Know About Her* with a famous shot of detergent and other consumer product cartons representing an urban wasteland, stating that he has to start again from square one. The press kit for *La Chinoise* includes the following statement: "Fifty years after the October Revolution, the American industry rules cinema the world over. . . . [W]e too should provoke two or three Vietnams within the vast Hollywood-Cinecittà-Mosfilms-Pinewood-etc. empire, and, both economically and aesthetically, struggling on two fronts as it were, create cinemas which are national, free, brotherly, comradely, and bonded in friendship" (N&M, 243 [translation modified]; B, 303). And although *Week-end* and *One Plus One/Sympathy for the Devil* (1968) may be best remembered, respectively, for the longest tracking shot (of a traffic jam) in film history, and the participation of the somewhat puzzled Rolling Stones, those films lead much further than their parodic treatment of consumer culture might suggest.

Between 1969 and 1972 Godard renounced what he saw as the bourgeois capitalist ideology of individual authorship, and his films were signed by the Dziga-Vertov Collective, based on his association with the Maoist Jean-Pierre Gorin. Yet by 1972, with *Tout va bien,* starring Jane Fonda and Yves Montand, the larger collective had reduced to the single Godard-Gorin couple. It was clear, however, that Godard was seeking in every way to create a different cinema, not just to make political films but, as he maintained, to make them "politically."[7] For financing he turned most often to television, but the producers were not always keen to have the films shown. His topics were internationalist – Britain, Prague, Italy, Palestine – but all within the framework of explicit Marxist critiques. His desire was to turn the film screen into a blackboard, an interface for active debate rather than a medium for passive consumption. With hindsight it is easy to say that this experiment by Godard failed, but then we would have to ask how success could be measured, given his avowed desire to renounce commercial cinema.[8] Godard continued to pursue such nonmercantile goals when, in 1974, he formed an association with Anne-Marie Miéville, and moved his operation from Paris to Grenoble, and from film to video, and for the following five years concentrated on programs designed for television or classroom use. His return to mainstream production with *Sauve qui peut (la vie)/Every Man for Himself* in 1979 was much heralded, and through the 1980s he again began to make films at the rate of about one per year. The fact that he is now at work on a somewhat open-ended video series entitled *Histoire(s) du cinéma* means on the one hand that he takes film to be a dying, or rather dead art, whose histories can now be written. The end of cinema is something, as he stated in 1965, the year of *Pierrot,* that he awaits "with optimism."[9] He harbors no illusions about reaching a wide audience – he never did, in fact, but was previously able to count on an informed and interested art house and college circuit reception – and certainly from the point of view of one who decried some thirty years ago the hegemony of Hollywood, little has changed to revitalize a monolithic, and hence ossified art form. On the other hand, Godard's continuing work means he will persist, however obstinately, to present his views, to insist that in spite of our consumption of images, a habit which seems to increase exponentially with each technological leap, we have not even begun to understand their meaning and functioning.

"OUI, BIEN SÛR; OUI, BIEN SÛR"

In a telling moment about halfway through *Pierrot le fou,* when the characters seem to have reached an impasse in their relationship, Pierrot asks Marianne whether she will ever leave him. She replies, *"Mais non, bien sûr"* ("Of course not"). *"Bien sûr?"* he persists. *"Oui, bien sûr"* ("Of course"). . . . *"Oui, bien sûr"* ("Of course"), she replies, repeating herself. Ferdinand's first question and Marianne's reply are spoken over the image of a pet fox. The second exchange is over an extreme close-up of Marianne's face. After each of the two *"oui, bien sûr"* replies, she turns from addressing Ferdinand and looks directly into the camera (*A-S*, 89; *W*, 61). Somewhere in there, between her first *"non"* and second two *"oui"*s, between her "no" and her "yes," between her first and second "yes," between him and her, or between her and the camera or audience, the truth should lie. But it remains an enigma, or at least divided into half-truths and lesser fractions whose disintegrating force structures the whole film and parallels the explosion of Ferdinand dynamiting himself at its end.

In French, a "yes" that contradicts a "no" is normally *"si"* rather than *"oui."* So Marianne does not really reverse her response from "no, of course (I'll never leave you)" to "yes, of course (I'll leave you)." Grammatically speaking, her *"oui, bien sûr"* reinforces her previous affirmation of fidelity. It can properly be translated as "no, of course not."[10] What I am suggesting, however, is that within the simple fact of a repetition, even one that seems to offer an exact replica, like a photographic image of itself, there falls the structure of difference that leads all the way to falsehood and contradiction. And it is telling that that repetition is punctuated by two "takes" of Marianne looking at the camera, as if the whole problematic and dilemma of photographic truth were being brought to bear on this cinematic moment, taking *Pierrot le fou* well out of the context of a romantic fugue and even of an existential quest, and reinserting it in the abyssal space of an interrogation concerning its own status as film.

In facing the camera and in "addressing" the audience not with her words, but with her gaze, Marianne might be looking to say any number of things about her and Pierrot, seeking an ally in the spectator as she does in fact with a direct address monologue later on. Thus we might understand her to be saying here, "Can't you see I'm telling the truth; why doesn't this jerk get it?"; "Can't you see I'm trapped into telling a lie? He understands so little about me we're bound to break up; he wants me to be faithful but on his terms"; "Whether I answer yes or no his jealousy will only confirm what he believes to be my infidelity." On the other hand, that same spectator will see subsequent images on this same surface that show her being unfaithful, and in effect leaving him. Hence it is as if she is repeating in her relationship to the spectator the same duplicity that she shows in her relationship to Ferdinand; we might even say we can see that insincerity in the look she gives us, and the film, in highlighting an equivocal image of Marianne as woman who is romantically desired object but also enigma, encourages and develops that idea.

Yet, as the film also makes abundantly clear, it is not just a simple story of Ferdinand and Marianne. From the beginning, any number of distanciation effects have broken the spectator's willing suspension of disbelief, not the least of these being the characters' acknowledgment, or denunciation, of the spectator's presence made explicit by their looking at the camera. When Ferdinand addresses the audience earlier, over his shoulder while driving the car, Marianne asks him who he is talking to and looks back only vaguely, as if she does not share or is not quite convinced by Ferdinand's desire to include the spectator in his drama (A-S, 86; W, 55). But now, in the double-take scene, it is as if she is coming to terms with that necessity, first, as I have just developed, in order to avail herself of a potential ally; but more importantly, in order to pose the question of truth and lies at the level of the film image itself, and not just within the diegesis represented in the film's images. I say that Marianne does this rather than that Godard does it because it is as if the quizzical look she previously gave to, or gave with respect to Ferdinand more than the spectator, has now become the duplicitous look of this scene, directly pointed at the spectator, and in which we can now read something like, "I don't know whether you and I are ready for this, but it isn't as simple as it looks." From this point of view, it is no longer just Marianne as character who is showing herself to be duplicitous but the image of Marianne as image. For there is a sort of reluctance mixed with the enigma of her look. She first looks down, almost bashfully, then raises her head to confront the camera, as if she were aware that she is not about to gain direct access to a sympathetic spectator but rather, or also, to deliver herself over to whatever image or manipulation of her image that the camera might opt for.

The moving image presents itself as a realist representation of the real world, one closer to reality itself than any other form – description, painting, photograph. It presents itself as a faithful copy of the world it represents. In using a repetition of word and image to express a doubt as much as a reinforcement, Godard's film focuses the spectator's attention on the difference that occurs within any repetition, even the most faithful copy. Once a copy is added to an original there is not just the original, plus the copy, but also the relation between them, which is *different* from either one or the other, even though one appears the same as the other. A different order of relations has been established, and indeed the term *original* has no sense unless it is used in the context of a real or potential copy.[11]

Thus Godard's refusal to preserve a seamless realism in his films must be understood less as willfulness on his part and more as a faithful attention to the reality of the cinematic image, the fact of its being a medium of relations, the space of difference within which there can occur everything from duplication to duplicity and lies. It is in this sense that I maintained that Marianne's stated or possible duplicity is finally that of the image as much as of the character. After all, once a character looks at the camera, she is saying not just whatever she says, but also, automatically, "I know you are a spectator in a movie theater looking at these images. I am an image; look at this image of me." Pierrot reinforces this when, as things fall apart, he also addresses the spectator in a monologue and explains haltingly that when Marianne says to him it is a fine day he only retains the appearance or image of her saying it is a fine day (*A-S*, 93; W, 74). The effect and emphasis of Godard's film, in providing this cinematic double-take, is thus to say, "Yes, of course I'll stick with you as spectator. I'll give you the illusion of looking at a real-life adventure, allowing you to lose yourself in it for a couple of hours. But hold on, look again, I have also to say that, yes, I would be unfaithful, I would be leaving you or letting you down, I would be duping you if I *didn't* remind you that these are *only* images you are looking at and not the real thing."

The duplicitous truth of the moving image, what, after Bazin, we might call the duplicity of its ontology,[12] or the way in which Godard, according to our reading of this series of shots, shows that truth to be divided within itself, is emblematic of other divisions or differences that work across the medium of the screen in *Pierrot le fou*. I have already made reference to the differences between the male and female protagonists, and on one level this is simply a function of the mismatch, incompatible personalities, competing goals and desires, opposite reactions to experiences, that make the film narrative bittersweet and lead ultimately to its tragic denouement. We see and hear about this in such scenes as that where the two protagonists mention their preferred tourist destinations (*A-S*, 84; W, 51); or explain what their opposing conceptions of "everything" are (*A-S*, 89–90; W, 63); or where Marianne says, "you speak to me with words and I look at you with emotions" (*A-S*, 89; cf. W, 62); or where Pierrot imposes his priority of serious literature over popular music (*A-S*, 90; W, 63–4). But within the context of film theory, the male-female difference is also about cinema, about the complexities of the cinematic gaze and mainstream film's decided penchant for positioning the female body as object of the gazes of both the camera and the male protagonist.[13] By means of her double glance at the camera, Marianne acknowledges her role as object of the gaze, informs the spectator that she knows he or she is looking – catching the voyeur in the act, as it were – and so begins to add a layer of questioning to her acceptance of that role. It is as if she were saying, "Yes, of course I like being looked at, but . . ." or "Yes, of course I know you are looking, but do you know what you are seeing?" and so on. Godard's films both collaborate with and exploit the objectification of the female figure in cinema, and it often becomes an explicit topic of discussion. For him the model of capitalism, exposed in a number of films such as *Vivre sa vie* and *Deux ou trois choses que je sais d'elle*, and again in *Sauve qui peut (la vie)*, is prostitution, and cinema is shown to function within the same structures of commodification of the (mostly) female body. In other cases, such as *Le Mépris,* he recasts the camera's voyeuristic gaze on the body of the sex symbol of the time, Brigitte Bardot, or, as in *British Sounds/See You at Mao* (1969), uses a sustained shot of a woman's pubic region to force the spectator to think about what he or she is doing in looking.

Within the narrative logic of *Pierrot,* Marianne does not get very far with her emancipation. She is hunted down and punished for it in classic fashion. However, we can retain the moment of her "yes, of course" double-take as opening the space of questioning regarding her role, reminding the spectator that possession by means of the gaze is an illusion, that within the medium of film are multiple layers of mediation, displacing the matter of duplicity once again from the woman herself to the camera's image of woman, which, in a sense, offers what it cannot deliver. For the satisfaction of an imaginary plenitude that possession of the image should provide for the spectator is in doubt once that supposed self-contained and all-inclusive plenitude is delivered twice: if it were sufficient unto itself it would have no need of repetition.

A further division made explicit in this scene is that between the language of images and speech. Since the invention of the talkies, the sound track has consistently been used in mainstream cinema to reinforce the image track, to provide the words that fit the movement of the actors' lips.[14] The images matched to Marianne's "yes, of course" follow that model, as does much of the other dialogue. But that second reply has also to be matched, and contrasted, with the first "yes, of course," that it echoes and calls into question, if not for the reasons I have elaborated on so far, then because of the contrasting image that accompanies the first reply, that of the fox. Now one might easily object that what mainstream cinema is in fact matching by means of its synchronizing of images and dialogue is the narrative or diegesis, and within that diegesis the fox has its place as a pet adopted by the couple in their desert isle existence. There is from that point of view every reason for the fox to appear in an image, and we are

Pierrot and Marianne, words and emotions

quite used to hearing parts of the dialogue over images other than faces with moving lips. But once Marianne's face and lips appear to repeat the "yes, of course" that we have already heard over the image of the fox, then in retrospect it is as if the fox had spoken the first time (both for Pierrot and Marianne), or else that Marianne, in speaking the second time (and by extension, perhaps, Pierrot also), was speaking like a fox, cunningly and slyly, expressing less her own cunning and slyness, and more the duplicity of that assumed relation of synchronicity between image and sound.

The image does not need sound – a silent film, photograph, or painting proves that – but realist cinema does, and, more particularly, narrative cinema does.[15] The dialogue, and often ambient sounds and music, help assure the smooth syntagmatic transition of image to image throughout a coherent narrative. Thus the dominant conception of realist cinema – narrative realist cinema – dictates an hierarchical combination of sounds, relations of spoken to written language, and so on, constituting the conventions that remain more or less strictly in force in most films, but which are brought into explicit focus, into critique and crisis, by the work of Godard.

A further rupture occurs in relations between image and sound track in a foreign film, namely the appearance of subtitles, adding unwelcome words to the image, and raising the problem of translation, of how best to render something like this double *"Oui, bien sûr,"* of what to include and what to leave out, and so on.[16] On the surface, the question of subtitles seems to be foreign to film in the strict sense, an accident of linguistic boundaries and international commerce, but in fact that is only true from the point of view of a dominant cinema operating within a dominant language, in our case a Hollywood that speaks English. In terms of world cinema we would have to conceive of subtitles as the norm rather than the exception. Godard's filmmaking has more than once alluded to this question, especially in *Le Mépris*, where he switches among English, French, German, and Italian, in order, it has been said, to frustrate the Italian practice of dubbing.[17] What I am suggesting, however, to return for the last time to the double-take, is that some sort of translation occurs between one *"Oui, bien sûr"* and another, even before they have to be translated into English. For let us not forget that the two *"oui, bien sûr"* statements follow a *"non, bien sûr,"* which, in spite of appearances, "means" the same thing. And of course it does and it does not. In spite of the strict grammatical logic I referred to earlier, it is also a linguistic fact that "no" does not mean the same as "yes." Language is posited on the possibility of maintaining differences as opposites; indeed any system of meaning functions on the principle of the differences between its signifiers, their noncoincidence as Saussure called it.[18] The change and repetition of Marianne's replies on the sound track thus set in place a structure of difference that becomes this complex configuration of repetitions and possible contradictions, contrasts between image and sound, angles and looks, tone and gesture, that is displayed in this scene and echoed throughout the film.[19] Through it, something moves or is translated across the signifying interface that is the screen and the sound system to inscribe difference even where there appears, or sounds, to be sameness, setting meaning as adrift as Pierrot and Marianne, introducing onto the film surface something irreducibly foreign.

Those effects are compounded once we consider the cinematic status of an image of written words, or of an image from a comic strip, or an advertisement, usually relegated to accidental or highly conventional incidences. In *Pierrot* it is almost as if those other forms were allowed to compete with the image serving the narrative. That narrative itself is presented more than once as an alternative between an adventure film or love story (*A-S*, 80; W, 45–6), between a Jules Verne novel or gangster movie (*A-S*, 90; W, 69), and at times the film has seemed to leave off that "story of the last romantic couple" in order to drift into a musical, a treatise, a documentary, a filmed play, and so on. Thus at whatever level we raise the question, or situate the analysis, we find that *Pierrot* unsettles the simple presentation of photographic truth, of narrative coherence, of psychological consistency, of semiotic systematicity, and of generic unity that we have been conditioned to presume and expect in watching film. It is everywhere saying, "yes, of course," "yes, of course," each time differently, and forcing the spectator into compounded double-takes that disorient his or her assurance concerning the images passing by on the screen.

For all those reasons, *Pierrot* might seem a very foreign film to many viewers, even before they hear its language and see its subtitles. But, in fact, it should be more familiar than ever. In the first place, as I suggested earlier, current audiences are more used than ever to "manipulations" of the image through their exposure to music video, rapid cutting, and tighter editing. In the second place, our culture is witnessing a transformation of the role of the image through new technologies, a revolutionizing of relations between verbal and iconic languages. In many ways Godard's desire for a cinematic blackboard can be seen as a 1960s prototype of the hypertext, inviting the spectator's active participation in the film's construction, offering points of reference and windows of information on various levels. Given our constant exposure to such visual effects, nothing should surprise us anymore. Thus the disorientation often provoked by Godard's film suggests that for all the technological and informational wizardry of recent years and its appropriation by audiovisual media in general, cinema has not really moved very far from the dominant matrices of the feature film that were installed in the years 1915 to 1930. There has been very little serious questioning of those matrices, such that however quaint or amateurish *Pierrot* might appear as we head toward the twenty-first century, it still preserves its ability to disconcert the viewer raised on the stringent diet of visual consumables that Hollywood seems determined to adhere to.

CONTEXTS AND PERSPECTIVES

The five essays in this volume present a variety of perspectives on *Pierrot le fou*. Richard Dienst's reflection posits a different kind of realism for Godard's film than that of movies based on the seamless recreation of a realistic, although fictional world on the screen. This is a reality – or as Dienst prefers, after Godard, a "life" – that does not come neatly constructed, but in fragments, above all these days in images. By the same token, though, the life presented to us is far from lacking in structure, and all the elements of the film that seem to disrupt its narrative momentum have their point, just as that narrative itself, or the story of the last romantic couple, has its point in the context of Velázquez, the Vietnam War, consumerism, and so on. Referring to the definition of cinema given by Samuel Fuller in the party scene, Dienst, again following Godard, calls that structure the "emotional unity" of the film, what finally makes *Pierrot* "an exploration of the ways life can be defined in terms of the desire for images."

In the second essay, Alan Williams provides specific details concerning some of the contexts that are relevant to a reading of the film. There is, first of all, the 1960s sentiment or sensibility, although Godard was by no means an enthusiastic supporter of the countercultural forms that began to develop during that period. Besides, we cannot assimilate the European experience of the 1960s to the American experience, although we can probably identify in that period the beginnings of the internationalization of (especially popular) culture that we recognize today. Williams emphasizes the importance of cinephilia, which, in the French context, represented something of a countercultural experience, as well as a growing political sensibility that was not without parallel, and conflict, with the positions of a group known as the situationists, for whom Godard's artistic activism appeared irredeemably bourgeois.

In the third essay, Jean-Louis Leutrat relates *Pierrot le fou* to two other films of the same period, *Une Femme est une femme/A Woman Is a Woman* (1961) and *Le Mépris*. What interests him in each case is not what we presume to be central to the film, but rather certain decentering or "ex-centering" effects, for in his view Godard seeks to avoid the single coherent and totalizing point of view that the camera, and mainstream cinema, seem to impose, in favor of a plurality of offcenter perspectives that are capable of leading the spectator along quite different lines of inquiry, a little like what I referred to earlier as the hypertextual, or window effect of his films. In the first part of his essay, Leutrat analyzes the role of the painted image in *Pierrot* (Jill Forbes also points to this) by means of a comparison with Luchino Visconti's famous 1954 film, *Senso*.[20] In his treatment of *Une Femme est une femme* Leutrat finds the credits alone to be worthy of close attention (Tom Conley shows that they are equally informative in *Pierrot*), whereas in *Le Mépris* it is the opening sequence that sets in play a whole other discursive, oral and aural network.

Tom Conley takes Godard at his word in treating his film as a blackboard, that is to say as a signifying interface on the basis of which the madness of the film's title refers less to its protagonist than to the play of signification itself. Or more precisely, he takes the film at its word(s), at the level of the maddeningly overwhelming volume of signifiers that it requires us to process, demonstrating the labyrinthine chains of sense making that are there to be followed should we dare. From Conley's point of view the ruptures I referred to earlier, between sound and image, between sound and writing, between different images, "threaten" as "interstices" or abysses within which meaning can fall, flee or fly, or crash and burn like Marianne and Pierrot. Conley's reading raises the question of what is in the film, what is put there by Godard, and what is brought to bear by a spectator or analyst. Such a question is in fact raised by the most timid reading, and for being impossible to resolve, constitutes the challenge and risk of writing about film, the risk of going too far, beyond the pale, that is the whole adventure and tragedy of *Pierrot*. In taking its signifiers, detail by detail, wherever he takes them, Conley never for all that departs from the explicit structures or raw data of the film.

We close the volume with an essay by Jill Forbes that returns to *Pierrot* in the context of film history, this time the wider context of French history and culture, and particularly film as it has developed since the New Wave. The difficulties of distribution in the American market faced by more recent foreign films, the inroads into the French film audience made by American cinema since the 1960s, and a certain Americanization of filmmaking by cinéastes such as Luc Besson have created a very different scene, but it is important to understand the extent to which Godard's work inserts itself into a local tradition. Thus Forbes reminds us that for all the apparent anti-Americanism of his work, there is in *Pierrot* a very evident fascination with American culture that later, in response to the escalation of the Vietnam War, became much more jaded. But, as she also points out, and as is echoed by other contributors, a number of factors specific to the French experience – Algeria and the politics of the postwar period, the rise of television, the importance of literature, and the experimentation with a popular literature represented by comics – make this a very French film, and make studying it, like any foreign language or cultural artifact, a complicated *cultural study*.

Pierrot le fou, like Godard's work in general, remains a milestone in the history of cinema, and an incredibly rich document for the student of film. It was, until relatively recently, unavailable on video and so has not received as much critical and classroom attention as other Godard classics. But it is more accessible than later films, and more polished yet still refreshingly and contrarily amateurish when compared with, say, *A bout de souffle*. It offers the student immediate entry to Godard's cinematic world while remaining sufficiently rich to demonstrate the complexity of the filmmaker's particular vision and his determination to remake the image from zero.

NOTES

1. At the 1997 Cannes festival, Godard presented the latest part of his ongoing project, *Histoire(s) du cinéma*, to very positive critical reaction from commentators, who were decrying the staleness and inability to surprise of many of the other films being presented, such as the mega-budgeted, star-vehicled, and special-effected *Fifth Element* (Luc Besson) or the ultraviolent *Assassin(s)* (Mathieu Kassovitz).
2. See Alan Williams, *Republic of Images* (Cambridge, MA: Harvard University Press, 1992), 381, for an explanation of the "accidental" invention of the jump cut.
3. "L'art à partir de la vie," B, 11. See Richard Dienst's essay for a different formulation of this question.
4. See B(ergala)'s division into the *Cahiers* years (1950–9), the Karina years (1960–7), the Maoist years (1968–74), the video years (1975–80), and the return to commercial cinema in 1980.
5. See Colin MacCabe, Mick Eaton, and Laura Mulvey, *Godard: Images, Sounds, Politics* (Bloomington: Indiana University Press, 1980), 84–90.
6. For further information, see Jill Forbes, *The Cinema in France: After the New Wave* (Bloomington: Indiana University Press, 1992), and Sylvia Harvey, *May '68 and Film Culture* (London: British Film Institute, 1980).
7. Jean-Luc Godard, "What is to be done?" *Afterimage* 1 (1970).
8. See again the analyses in MacCabe et al., *Godard: Images, Sounds, Politics*, 50–77.
9. "Questionnaire aux cinéastes français," *Cahiers du cinéma* 161–2 (1965), reprinted in N&M, 210; B, 257. Jonathan Rosenbaum has compared the *Histoire(s) du cinéma* project with *Finnegan's Wake*, coming after the end of cinema just as James Joyce's masterwork "situates itself at some theoretical stage after the end of the English language as we know it" ("Trailer for Godard's *Histoires du cinéma*," *Trafic* 21 [1997]: 18).
10. The Whitehead translation reads as follows: M: "No, of course, not." F: "Of course, not?" M: "Yes, of course. . . . Yes, of course . . ." (W, 61). The subtitles differ: M: "Of course I won't." F: "Of course?" M: "Of course . . ." M: "Yes . . . of course."
11. For a development of this argument, see Peter Brunette and David Wills, *Screen/Play: Derrida and Film Theory* (Princeton: Princeton University Press, 1989), 68–75.
12. Cf. André Bazin, "The Ontology of the Photographic Image," in

What Is Cinema? Vol. 1, trans. Hugh Gray (Berkeley: University of California Press, 1967), 9–16.

13. See the seminal article by Laura Mulvey, "Male Pleasure and Narrative Cinema," and, for example, the range of other analyses also included in Constance Penley (ed.), *Feminism and Film Theory* (New York: Routledge, 1988).

14. The sound track does not, of course, reduce to dialogue. For discussion of this, particularly as it relates to Godard, see Alan Williams, "Godard's Use of Sound," *Camera Obscura* 8–10 (1982): 199–208 (reprinted in Elisabeth Weiss and John Belton [eds.], *Film Sound: Theory and Practice* [New York: Columbia University Press, 1986], 332–45); and my "Carmen: Sound/Effect," *Cinema Journal* 25, 4 (1986): 33–43, and "Representing Silence (in Godard)," in Bruce Merry (ed.), *Essays in Honour of Keith Val Sinclair* (Townsville: James Cook University Press, 1991), 180–92.

15. This is not the same as saying that an image does not need discourse of some sort, usually writing, in our culture. See Jacques Derrida, *The Truth in Painting,* trans. Geoff Bennington and Ian McLeod (Chicago: University of Chicago Press, 1987).

16. I have discussed this in some detail in "The French Remark: *Breathless* and Cinematic Citationality," in Andrew Horton and Stuart McDougal (eds.), *Play It Again Sam: Retakes on Remakes* (Berkeley and Los Angeles: University of California Press, 1998).

17. James Monaco, *The New Wave* (New York: Oxford University Press, 1976), 137–8.

18. "A segment of language can never in the final analysis be based on anything except its noncoincidence with the rest." Ferdinand de Saussure, *Course in General Linguistics,* trans. Wade Baskin (New York: McGraw-Hill, 1966), 118.

19. We could analyze other cases of repeated dialogue in the film in terms of this structure of difference or rupture. Examples would be the complicated story ("all mixed up" as the subtitles have it [cf. *A-S,* 79–80; W, 42–3]) as Pierrot and Marianne flee the Paris apartment, or Marianne's refrain of boredom ("What am I gonna do? I don't know what to do" [*A-S,* 89–90; W, 62–3]) that has at its center the telling difference in conceptions of "everything," or Pierrot's recitation of Frederico Garcia Lorca's lines as he sits on the railway tracks and "rehearses" his suicide (*A-S,* 97; W, 81).

20. *Senso,* the story of a Venetian countess's passion for an enemy Austrian officer, was controversial for its reassessment of both the history of the Italian reunification and neorealist cinematic practice, but widely acclaimed for its use of color.

RICHARD DIENST

1 The Imaginary Element

LIFE + CINEMA

With Godard, making images looks so easy. Each of his films, no matter what else it does, offers an extensive demonstration of technique, as if it wants to be more than merely "reflexive" about itself – instead, it sets out to teach you how it was made. Making a film is to be treated as a practical extension of watching films – it seems to be nothing more than a matter of learning how to use a camera, finding some people who want to act, and coming up with a story as you go along. If there is no dialogue, a poem will work just as well. If you need a strong image to amplify a scene, find a painting or a comic strip. Quote everything that comes to mind. As for a script, there is no need for a grand plan because something is always bound to happen. To those who know how to let the unforeseeable happen, nothing is fortuitous. You make a film using whatever you have ready at hand – collaborators, equipment, the places you can go, the time you have to spare – but in the end you make a film in order to transform all of that into something quite different. It is not a question of conjuring up the enigmatic glow of art, nor a question of making a cut-rate version of what the industry already produces, nor even a question of doggedly telling the truth; you make a film Godard's way because you want to prove that it is possible to live a certain kind of life, where your politics, work habits, personal relationships, cash flow, and all your cultural tastes and inheritances can come into play at any given moment.

On second thought, things are not so simple. If Godard were merely promoting a do-it-yourself aesthetic, we would not need to watch his films at all, let alone pay careful attention to their textures and dynamics. And if these films were nothing but lightly veiled slices of life from the 1960s Parisian avant-garde, there would be no reason to think that this work offers a radical perspective still powerful today. However much Godard's early films may have served as inspiration to later filmmakers, or offered lifestyle role models to generations of audiences, our task here is to put these lasting attractions to a more critical test. If there is something about Godard's work that provokes us to develop an especially active and productive relationship to the practice of cinema, we ought to be able to locate the images that convey this challenge. By the same token, if these films somehow raise the possibility of living some other kind of life, whether that hope is glimpsed through the figure of the spontaneous auteur or in the secondhand idiom of Hollywood fantasy, we ought to be able to examine how Godard's work makes this sense of possibility visible.

It is not at all obvious that any film would try so directly to teach us how to live, yet with *Pierrot le fou* we have a film that insistently turns "cinema" and "life" into problems demanding solutions. We see Belmondo asking what cinema really is (*A-S*, 75; W, 28); we hear Anna[1] wishing that life could be as unified, clear, and logical as a book (*A-S*, 76; W, 36); we see the surface of the film and the shape of the characters broken into so many pieces that we begin to wonder what could hold it all together. But *Pierrot* is not "about" cinema, and it would be hard to say it is "about" life: it is, as Godard says, "an attempt at cinema" that "reminds us that one must attempt to live" (N&M, 215; B, 263). That sounds just right, but there is still nothing obvious about the meaning of these words or the relationship between them. It is common to hear everybody talk about how life becomes like cinema, or how cinema becomes like life, or how one builds on the other, or escapes it. Through these clichés, each word has become the unspoken alibi of the other. We are used to the idea that cinema shows us what life cannot see for itself; when cinema ends, life is supposed to begin again. Perhaps we ought to be suspicious of this neat symmetry. The idea of cinema has lost its saving power, its innocent modernity, that once seemed to infuse it, just as the idea of life has lost the libidinal and existential attraction that once surrounded its every invocation. But for Godard these words have remained indispensable.[2] In *Pierrot*, he brings them forward at the same time, turning such grand but vague ideas into strange vibrant objects – literally flashing signs – that beckon to us from the screen. Is this *cinema* (*A-S*, 100; W, 91)? Is this *life* (*A-S*, 85, 86; W, 54, 56)? Perhaps, as we will see, these are two names for the same impulse or element, even if between them there is all the difference in the world.

THE PIERROT COMPLEX

In a far-reaching and intriguing interview conducted by *Cahiers du cinéma* just after he had completed *Pierrot*, Godard found himself being cross-examined on a wide range of topics, from the details of his filmmaking technique to his grandest artistic claims. The text of this interview, like many others before and since, proves Godard to be a brilliant talker, as provocative and unpredictable on the page as he is with his films. His responses – by turns cynical, chatty, and polemical – are full of blunt aphorisms, startling quotations, and sweeping statements of principle. He speaks as if he were trying to turn passing ideas and the swirl of conversation into lasting expressions of thought. Not only that: the interview seems to have struck a creative nerve, because soon afterward Godard went on to write his own text to accompany it, a kind of prose poem entitled *"Pierrot* mon ami," set to a more individualized and more delirious poetic tune. Taken together with the film, these texts form a kind of Pierrot complex, a set of variations on a theme, each one demonstrating the way Godard blurs the usual distinctions between seeing, saying, and thinking.[3]

On the page, he tries to shape his phrases like pictures, strings of words caught together in a snapshot grammar, inflected with the peculiar tones of a highly colored literary language. Reading these texts can seem a lot like watching his films: in both cases Godard encourages us to check images against ideas until the acts of seeing and thinking overlap each other in the same flow. Given that Godard's films always include "textual" moments (where the interruption of images by words calls for commentary and analysis), it is not surprising that there should be passages of cinema (lyrical, opaque, sometimes oneiric) crossing through his written texts. Indeed, the critical and poetic impulses in his work come to be expressed in words and images alike. As he says in relation to a later film, "I make my films not only when I'm shooting, but as I dream, eat, read, talk to you."[4] These outpourings are not the ramblings of a self-absorbed aesthete; they are instead the deliberate exercises of someone trying to intervene in the ongoing public construction of the world. They offer lessons in *seeing as a political act*. These lessons concern something I will call "attitude," a word that evokes both the playacting sense in which everybody puts on a performance as a social being, and the more conventional sense of the word as opinion, perspective, orientation, or outlook. Thus "attitude" signals the way in which we embody, in a given posture, both our sense of individual agency and our relationships to those around us.

It is here, in the ceaseless production of cinema + life, that we should look for Godard's understanding of history. It will not be easy. Godard's early films seem entirely caught up in their own moment; they are so "contemporary" that "history" would only enter the picture afterward, when the newness of the films has worn off and they can be treated as documentary or cultural relics of a bygone time. But that is not the kind of history which concerns us here. Instead, we will assemble a concept of history out of the tension Godard creates between cinema and life, using all the complexities of his work. Godard knows how to bring out the historical dimensions of whatever he films; throughout his career, he has tried to diffract history, to make images that bend the rays of historical events and brush against the edges of lived experience. History zooms in and out, at one moment close and vibrant (like de Gaulle's parade in *A bout de souffle/Breathless* [1960]) and in the next distant and enigmatic (like the offscreen protest suicide in *Masculin Féminin/Masculine Feminine* [1966]). History includes the tangible aftershocks of grand events (Vietnam, Algeria) as well as the ephemeral markers of cultural life under capitalism (pop songs, advertisements). But perhaps these mixed signals are the way history always appears, in cinema as in life: through a grid of images that both pattern and scatter the shape of what we later reconstruct as historical events. All images are surely stamped with history, and all history is indelibly stamped by imaginary powers. As Walter Benjamin wrote, "History breaks down into images, not into stories."[5] With a little rearranging, Benjamin's statement could serve as a basic description of Godard's method: to break down stories into images and to break down images into history – in order to rebuild new kinds of images and new kinds of stories. So if Godard does not mention history alongside cinema and life, that is because it is already there – although equally problematic and equally elusive – in those other concepts. Instead of assuming that history is some kind of ultimately metaphysical notion, it would be more fitting to say that the materials of history are necessarily available in what we see and what we live, even if we often don't know how to retrieve them; so that "cinema" and "life" come to serve as the simplest available frames in which to collect and contain all those passing events we could not otherwise recognize and reclaim.

CINEMATIC LOVE

When Godard announces that he wants to test the limits of "cinema" and "life," the stakes are high and the challenge is radical. Yet he is not one of those unrelentingly "critical" artists who would insist on rubbing everybody's noses in their perpetual failure to make sense of the world. There is a persistent affirmation in Godard's work, and it can be traced to his insistence on the "unity" of ideas, images, and sounds. But, as we will see, this "unity" is called into question over and over again. It is never exactly where you would expect to find it, neither in the story line nor in the stacks of images and layers of sound cut together by montage; neither in "the world" pieced together within the film nor in "the world" that is supposed to exist beyond it; neither in the people presented for our inspection nor in the people who remain out of view. His films keep looking in each of these directions, but no "unity" is to be found there, rather only a "solidarity" of visual, aural, and conceptual materials in which we, as spectators, can participate. He promises us, through the narrative and in the montage, a cinematic love of the world. For Godard, this love – which is neither sentimental nor nostalgic – is the most urgent kind of affect: intimate and political at the same time.

How can a film so insistent about "life" and "emotion," so wrapped up in the course of a romance, turn out to be a "political" film? Clearly all these terms are up for grabs, and the first thing we have to notice is that Godard combines the bluntest political references with the tenderest romantic encounters. In the *Cahiers* interview, one of the journalists describes this mixture as an aesthetic flaw. His criticism is disappointingly familiar. The journalist observes, "Everytime actuality comes up in the film, one gets the impression of a rupture in the mood" (N&M, 224; B, 269). Godard defends himself, arguing that the references to current events were justified by the drama between Anna and Belmondo. But the interviewers persist: "It is often said that dragging politics like this into a story such as the Anna-Belmondo adventure is dilettantism" (N&M, 225; B, 269). The reproach is clear: one should not mix a love story with politics. It would seem that a few explicitly violent scenes and an insistent subtext (the details of which we investigate later) are enough to spoil the illusion of romantic adventure; for the sensitive moviegoer, Godard's loose weave of references to wars and political groups proves that he is not really committed to his love story. (Yet he is not accused of being committed to some political program, either.) All these references are "dilettantish"

Nature and romance

because they are never drawn up for judgment; precisely because these images and events cannot be located in motives or positions, they remain that much more pervasive, serving as disturbing reminders of some other world that cuts into and sometimes rules over the one being made onscreen. In this sense, whatever escapes the spell of romance would appear to be "political," whether it is a radio news broadcast, an encounter with American tourists, or a subplot somehow dealing with gunrunning. "Politics," in other words, would be everything we would have to forget in order to follow the course of the film.

But Godard does not accept this criticism at all. Over and over again, his films destroy these distinctions and evaluations – especially the idea that cinema should somehow be more pure, more coherent, and more balanced than everyday life. To his interviewers he responds, "One may feel that in *Pierrot* the unity is purely emotional, and point out that something does not fit the emotional unity; but simply to say that politics have no right to be there is pointless since they are part of the emotional unity" (N&M, 225; B, 270). As long as romance appears to be the ultimate narrative or affective focal point, the political references can be tolerated only if they somehow comment on the course of love – as symbolic reminders of violence, for example, or as a measure of obstacles to be overcome – but once the whole story is understood in terms of a Godardian "emotional unity" it becomes possible to turn around all these criticisms, and to think of the ways this melancholy love story can serve as a commentary on contemporary politics. Instead of complaining about a few "contaminating" political elements, we could just as well treat the lyrically romantic scenes as the most explicitly political moments of the story. (The first scene in the car, when Anna and Belmondo rekindle their love after hearing the radio report of a massacre in Vietnam [A-S, 76; W, 36–7], is bearable only because their emotions for each other seem to grow out of a moment of compassion for the anonymous dead.) This reversal of perspective cannot be a simple leveling out: it is not enough to switch the accents from one part of the film to another. We don't want to replace the old-fashioned aesthetic standards of the *Cahiers* interviewers with an equally old-fashioned polemical litmus test. The "romance" of the film, like its "political" sympathies, does not reside strictly in the plot or in the characters: such issues emerge on another plane, on another scale, through the folds of Godard's composition. If Godard's formal strategy succeeds – and this is the wager of modernist practice – the energies ordinarily invested in a love story or a political intrigue would be cut loose, available for some other kind of critical and artistic operation. It is only by *disengaging* the romance from Anna and Belmondo, and by *distancing* the political coordinates from the plot, that Godard is able to examine romantic involvements and political ideas as historical problems.[6]

EMOTION AND MOTION

Thus the "emotional unity" of a film would be precisely its *form*, that is, both the integrity of its composition and the range of its imaginary connections. Yet, as Marxist aestheticians since Lukács have argued, a "form" should be recognized as a "form-problem," as the provisional "solution" executed in a specifically artistic medium to historical dilemmas that would remain unrecognized or insoluble in any other sphere.[7] The problem of cinematic form, therefore, revolves around this simple question: What binds images together? Is it the act of spectatorship? Is it the technological process of filming? Is it the irreducible materiality and worldliness of the images themselves? In *Pierrot*, Godard's sweeping answer – *c'est l'émotion* – is in fact delivered twice, in the course of a three-way conversation among Belmondo, Samuel Fuller, and a translator (*A-S*, 75; W, 28–33). The battling forces Godard designates as "emotion" must operate on a grand scale: they cannot be assigned exclusively to an actor, or to the director, or to the audience. "Emotion" would have to be the common force of all imaginary movements: it is what happens whenever images are drawn together, and in that sense "emotion" always brings both the prospect of unification as well as the threat of disorientation and uncertainty. Emotion makes you feel alive only by opening your borders to the energies of other lives: in this sense, it would be a mistake to take your emotions "personally," as though these sensations related only to you: in the moment of emotional transport, there sparks an image.

In "Pierrot mon ami" Godard writes that the imaginary disturbance known as "emotion" is a physical process: "This double movement, which projects us toward others at the same time as it really takes us back to ourselves, physically defines the cinema" (N&M, 215; B, 263). Here, "emotional unity" turns out to be both a bodily and an ethical dilemma. A film does not work on our senses passively, but it presents us with a bundle of images in which we find ourselves caught. If neither our perceptions nor the images onscreen ever achieve a state of complete composure, we have to figure out when to piece together a seeing "self" and when to piece together the "others" being seen – and each act is a kind of montage, loosely reciprocal and always provisional. (Belmondo becomes fed up with the bourgeois party at the moment when he feels most broken apart: his eyes, a "machine for seeing," are disconnected from his machines for hearing, for speaking [A-S, 75; W, 33–4].) Godard tries to heighten the intensity of this to-and-fro image making. By unexpectedly breaking down images into components – the jump cuts, the sudden washes of color – Godard "decomposes" what might otherwise be taken as a settled, natural picture. Such "defamiliarization" always leads back to the simplest kind of materialist perception, as demonstrated in a famous joke from the *Cahiers* interview. The journalist has observed, "there is a great deal of blood" in the film. But Godard replies, "Not blood, red" (N&M, 217; B, 264). Before it can be *read* as blood, the red must be *seen* as red. Slowing down, looking closely, holding off the temptation to decide the meaning of everything right away: these are the operations through which Godard insists that we take responsibility for what we see. The parameters of this responsibility can change minute by minute: as images pass by onscreen, whether joined together or not, they open up new connections, new fields of reference, and the act of seeing becomes ineluctably implicated in a jumble of sexual, political, and historical relationships. Rather than shying away, the spectator must embrace this movement toward others through the element of images. "All experiences are moral experiences," said Nietzsche, arguing that the simplest act of perception required a kind of decision and commitment.[8] The "battle" of cinema is waged over the way we have to choose our place in the world opened by images, and any film that cannot first dislodge us cannot bring us back to new knowledge either. In that sense, Godard does not want to lead us to a knowledge based on the mere fusion of cinema and life – that would be tantamount to a religion based on cinematic experience – but rather to propel us out of that duality, toward a knowledge of what I am calling history, the entanglement of seeing and living as the emergence of a critical and creative attitude. Although this radical position has been reiterated over the course of the twentieth century by theatrical predecessors like Brecht and theoretical descendants like MacCabe, Heath, and Wollen,[9] it has not lost its force, even if it has lost its once formidable place in the cultural landscape.

THE TRAPPINGS OF CINEMA

To judge by the variations within the *Pierrot* complex, Godard had reached a well-developed sense of the range of aesthetic and political material he wanted to treat, and it would be possible to trace throughout his later work (all the way up to the present) a series of variations and repetitions of the material presented here. (Typically, however, Godard insists that he had no idea how *Pierrot* would turn out, just a week before shooting began.[10]) It would be no exaggeration to say that Godard wanted to pack as much as possible into the film: "at that time for me it was a matter of spreading out everything that could be put in the lens [dans l'objectif]: Marianne, Anna Karina, a little dwarf, Vietnam, finally everything that might come to mind at that time."[11] Insofar as we can speak of distinct characters and a coherent story line, these items may be nothing more than the minimal supports on which a great deal of referential weight has to be placed. Instead of stripping down the immense variety of the images in order to assemble things like a plot, plausible motives, and a suitably symbolic set of interpretations, it would be much more in keeping with Godard's attitude to let the usual critical guidelines fall away, and deal with the film as an exercise in the multiple transcriptions of a complex historical domain. It is hard to know what to call the formal area being built up here: its imaginary scheme would have to be defined not just by the terrain that the characters inhabit and traverse, but also by the ideal spaces configured by their words (the diary, the literary quotations), by the director's seemingly capricious citations (two women playing tennis at the very beginning, a Renoir painting), and by the touches of "actuality" (newsreels of Vietnam, torture methods from the Algerian war, the arms trade to Yemen, Angola, and the Congo), all of which pass in and out of sight without letting themselves be pinned down.

So we are offered the trappings of cinema – a blending of recognizable formal building blocks with whatever gets trapped by the camera and the projector. Two intriguing statements, both from "Pierrot mon ami," can serve as useful descriptions of this seemingly aleatory labor of construction. The first sounds like a Zen riddle: "two shots which follow each other do not necessarily follow each other. The same goes for two shots which do not follow each other" (N&M, 215; B, 263). This ought to be a tremendously liberating idea: on one hand, it relieves us of having to base all our decisions about meaning on mere sequence. To follow in time or in space is not always to follow the course of a thought. Images may be ordered according to some logic, but we are not bound to follow that logic when we retrace the course of images. On the other hand, this is not an endorsement of chaos. There is not necessarily any special value in disruption, in shots that do not fol-

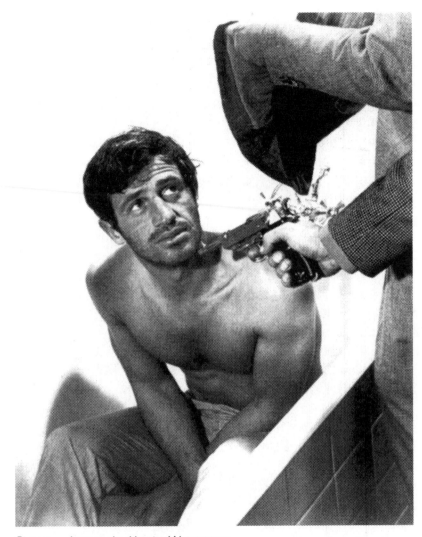

Pierrot undergoes the Algerian War torture

low: images have to be made and seen in relation to each other, even if those relationships do not all run along the same current. But it is only through the possibility of not-following that each image can retain its own specific weight. The proper critical question thus becomes "What does *this* have to do with *that?*" The scheme Godard sketches here resembles Benjamin's "constellation," in which the traces and fragments of images are shaped into arcs of figuration without either losing their own specificity or finishing the design of the whole. As Professor Pluggy (played by Godard himself) puts it in *King Lear* (1987) (more than twenty years after *Pierrot*), "An image is not strong because it is brutal or fantastic, but because the association of ideas is distant and true." A constellation becomes true only because it keeps the distances it draws together. Only in that way can we keep our bearings in a world where the horizon keeps moving to and fro. Now the original riddle has become a bit more clear: what had seemed to be a paradox about the inevitable disconnection of images becomes instead the principle by which they should be assembled by the filmmaker and the spectator alike. We have to follow the rule of that which does not always follow. And Godard would insist that this rule – which describes the opening up of montage to possibility, and which spells the end of generic and thematic recipes – can only be learned in seeing, not in speaking, not in writing.[12]

The second statement from "Pierrot mon ami" returns us more directly to the ethical demand that Godard locates within cinema's dynamics: "the only great problem with cinema seems to me more and more with each film when and why to start a shot and when and why to stop it. Life, in other words, fills the screen as a tap fills a bath which is simultaneously emptying at the same rate at the same time" (N&M, 214; B, 262). It sounds as if the whole conflict between cinema and life is restaged in every shot: if a shot always begins with a violent irruption, the splash of cinema into the living world, then sooner or later, if it is left running too long, it will spring a leak in the world and drain it of its energy, leaving us with nothing but cinema. Thus the economy of the shot would also govern the economy of the whole film. Ideally, a film would be pitched at the pace of living, whatever that may be, but it would have to be the pace set by at least two agents, as in a race, a game, or a fight. That is why Belmondo and Anna are both crucial structural components and ultimately dispensable place-holders. They become only substantial enough to keep up the flow, but not so "three dimensional" that they absorb the currents which pass through them. For if we make the mistake of attributing the life of the film to their blinded flight rather than our awakening vision, it will lead only to the death of the imaginary impulse. The catastrophic conclusion is more than a way to break any temptation we might have had to identify with them: it is yet another decomposition, this time operating in the narrative form, that dissolves these imaginary compositions back into the elements which made them (and again, color plays its role – Anna gets her death in red; Belmondo's comes in blue).

By declining to read more thoroughly into these characters and this story line, I do not mean to suggest that *Pierrot le fou* falls apart into senselessness if you look at it too closely. It makes a great deal of sense every step of the way. Evidently, somewhere between starting and ending his shots, Godard found room for efficient storytelling, charming musical set pieces, virtuoso jokes, and other pleasures of the cinematic tradition. But when the film is read as just one part of the *Pierrot* complex, cross-cut with Godard's theories and prose poetry, its imaginary drive becomes even more expansive, more complicated, and somehow much more useful. With repeated viewings, the film does not shrink to the dimensions of the two doomed characters, but rather seems to keep growing, taking on the dimensions of an ever-regenerating aesthetic and historical event. Indeed, *Pierrot* was the film that gave Godard a renewed sense of purpose after years of exhausting work. As he put it in the *Cahiers* interview, "Cinema is optimistic because everything is always possible, nothing is ever prohibited: all you need is to be in touch with life" (N&M, 233; B, 278). Even if cinema can be rejuvenated and liberated by seeking contact with something called life, it is still not clear how we will know life when we see it. Is "life" a trope, a rhythm, a raw material, a ground (either in the foreground or background), a slipstream of chance, or the reliable bedrock of understanding? What must "life" be, if it needs images so badly? To that seemingly ineffable question we now turn.

IMAGINING LIFE

All the talk about life in the film faithfully echoes the tenor of Godard's comments in print. "Life" is an elusive but unquestioned good, stirring out there somewhere, already underway. ("True life is elsewhere," Anna murmurs, evoking Rimbaud [*A-S*, 86; cf. W, 56].) What is more, Godard has continued to use this well-worn language, although he has expanded the terminology to accommodate his sharpened political sensibilities. For example, around the time of *Sauve qui peut (la vie)/Every Man for Himself* (1979), he wrote, "Cinema is a laboratory of life; one can find everything there, relations of production, hatreds, loves, parent-child and worker-boss relationships, and moreover all of this operates in order to manufacture an artistic good, it is the paradise for the study of life while living it" (B, 449). Seen from this later vantage point, *Pierrot* emphatically demonstrates the capacity of cinema to teach us about the constraining and alienating dimensions of life, along with the possibilities of living otherwise. The characters are not there to be criticized or emulated, the settings are not there to repel or entice us, and the plot is not there to offer a moral or to show us the way of all things: instead, by watching how these lives unfold, always in fits and starts, we learn that we have not yet learned how to live.[13]

To take the film at its word, we would have to say that cinema teaches us not life itself – which can never be glimpsed anyway – but rather the desire to live. Belmondo makes a pun on these words: *J'avais envie, j'étais en vie* ("I felt desire, I was alive") translated in the subtitles as "To want something, you have to be alive" (*A-S*, 76; cf. W, 35). Although it may seem like an ancient cliché to define life as a desire, here that desire cannot be grasped in itself: it must pass by way of cinema. Thus *Pierrot* can be understood as an exploration of the ways life can be defined in terms of the desire for images. This desire is not always healthy – as the girdle advertisement and the consumerist stupor at the party indicate – but it is always the force of movement in the film, and sometimes it reaches delirious and joyous speeds, as when they first reach the ocean, and Belmondo exclaims, "Life may be sad, but it's always beautiful. Suddenly I feel free" (*A-S*, 86; W, 56). That trace of melancholy arises because the most exultant desires are always joined to broken and corrupted ones: *Pierrot* proves it. Rather than "desires," then, which are all too easily channeled into commodity fetishism and ego trips, we should speak about *wishes,* and wishes must be seen in order to have a chance to enter life.

Two great intellectual currents of our era can be understood as attempts to theorize wishes, in order to put them somehow into practice. Psychoanalysis, in all its analytic and interpretive procedures, understands the exchange between the unconscious and the practice of life as a fundamentally imaginary transaction, and Marxist critique understands social life as a whole in terms of the mobilization of wishes through both ideological lures and utopian hopes. In each set of critical terms, the labor of being alive requires a ceaseless imaginary passage between the provisional satisfaction of clipped desires and the reemergence of fresh wishes. Thus "life" cannot be understood as a vague longing or a merely organic pulse, it is not "naked" or elemental or immaterial; instead, it is the images which are elemental: the images of each other that we pass back and forth, the images that compose the milieu in which we move, the images we let stand for other images. The life taught by cinema can never be extracted from its imaginary element: it must be grasped as something material but in motion; driven by the vicissitudes of light but drawn together by the demands of form; shaped by relationships without being seized by any single configuration; manifested as an attitude and posture toward others rather than a stance or a pose for ourselves. In this way we come to learn about seeing the imaginary possibilities and powers that surround us, which are all too often colonized and exhausted by the attempt to realize the wishes invested in them. The desire for images may be at work in all spheres of life, but for Godard it is bound up with the forms of life particular to his time and ours, a capitalist world system that seems ever less willing to allow the expression of collective wishes. Instead of despairing over the inadequacy of this imaginary labor, Godard himself finds hope in it: "Yes. One must film, talk about everything. Everything remains to be done" (N&M, 234; B, 280). It would be a great artistic and political coup if *Pierrot le fou* could still offer that sense of a future to cinema, or to life. Godard teaches us that images, on screen and in thought, are powerful because they bring forth *what remains to be seen*: making visible *both* what has been left over *and* what has yet to emerge.

NOTES

1. I refer to the main characters as Anna and Belmondo, following Godard's practice in his writings. (Obviously, to use the script names – Marianne and Ferdinand – would prejudice issues of naming that can only be acknowledged by being left open.)
2. On some other occasion it would be worthwhile to examine the figure of the homegrown *Cahiers* auteur within the tradition of twentieth-century aesthetic/political movements (with their distinctive small-group dynamics and peculiar compromises with money and power). In Godard's case, it would be necessary to pay special attention to his literary reference points: not just the books mentioned in the films, but the personal canon of novelists (which would include, on the topic of "life," Sartre and D. H. Lawrence). For a sympathetic account of this tradition, see the thinker whose work on Godard is becoming the standard reference: Gilles Deleuze, "Literature and Life," *Critical Inquiry* 23 (1997): 225–30.
3. "*Pierrot* My Friend" and "Let's Talk About *Pierrot*," N&M, 213–34; B, 259–80.
4. "One Should Put Everything into a Film," N&M, 238; B, 295.
5. Walter Benjamin, "N [Theoretics of Knowledge; Theory of Progress]," trans. Leigh Hafrey and Richard Sieburth, *The Philosophical Forum* 15, 1–2 (1983–4): 25. This piece is an excerpt from Benjamin's unfinished *Passagenwerk* compilation, which offers a wealth of insight into the relationship between images and historical thinking.
6. For insight into Godard's evolving attitudes toward history, see the 1988 interview with Serge Daney: "Godard Makes [Hi]stories," in Raymond Bellour and Mary Lea Bandy (eds.), *Jean-Luc Godard, Son +*

Image 1974–1991 (New York: Museum of Modern Art, 1992), 159–67.

7. For a treatment of the notion of a "form-problem" in the context of cinema studies, see Fredric Jameson, "The Existence of Italy," in his *Signatures of the Visible* (New York: Routledge, 1990), 162–4.

8. Friedrich Nietzsche, *The Gay Science*, trans. Walter Kaufman (New York: Vintage, 1974). The whole passage reads: "*How far the moral sphere extends*. – As soon as we see a new image, we immediately construct it with the aid of all our previous experiences, *depending on the degree* of our honesty and justice. All experiences are moral experiences, even in the realm of sense perception" (173–4).

9. For examples of work in this tradition, see Bertolt Brecht, *Brecht on Theatre*, trans. John Willett (New York: Hill and Wang, 1964); Colin MacCabe, Mick Eaton, and Laura Mulvey, *Godard: Images, Sounds, Politics* (Bloomington: Indiana University Press, 1980), a work as enjoyable and provocative as a Godard film; Stephen Heath, "Lessons from Brecht," *Screen* 15, 2 (1974): 103–28; Peter Wollen, "Godard and Counter-Cinema: *Vent d'Est*," in *Readings and Writings* (London: Verso Editions, 1982), 79–91.

10. Jean-Luc Godard, *Introduction à une véritable histoire du cinéma* (Paris: Éditions Albatros, 1980), 147.

11. Ibid.

12. This is an echo of one of his scribbled definitions: "montage: seeing only what can be seen (not said, not written)" (*Introduction à une véritable histoire du cinéma*, 155). The primacy Godard accords to the visual is not therefore based on its sensory immediacy, but on the powers of thought that (according to his unsystematic formulations) can only be exercised through the processes of visuality.

13. This phrase is a deliberate echo of the opening of Jacques Derrida's *Spectres of Marx* (New York: Routledge, 1994): "Someone, you or me, comes forward and says: *I would like to learn how to live finally*" (xvii). If Godard, like Derrida, wants to remain faithful to a certain Marxism by proposing lessons meant "to help broadly in living," it is important to remember that he also distanced himself from the institutional Marxisms of his day. (The quoted phrase is from *"Pierrot* mon ami" [N&M, 215; B, 263].)

In the scene when Anna and Belmondo gaze at the moon, we hear Belmondo describe how the man in the moon has been driven out by cosmonauts bringing Lenin and astronauts bringing Coca-Cola (*A-S*, 88; W, 58). His comment recalls the alternate title of *Masculin Féminin*: "The Children of Marx and Coca-Cola." These phrases point directly to a "neither Washington nor Moscow" political stance that had a highly visible place in French culture nearly twenty years before Godard's film. In the late 1940s, for example, Sartre's short-lived political party had been based on such a "neither/nor" position, and we can hear a more striking presage in a statement by André Breton in December 1948: "It's the rival imperialism of Coca-Cola and disfigured Marxism that we must, by the quickest means possible, render incapable of consuming and sacrificing our lives" (quoted in Mark Polizzotti, *Revolution of the Mind: The Life of André Breton* [New York: Farrar Straus Giroux, 1995]), 558. From our historical vantage point we should marvel at the misshapen metonymies here: Western capitalism being summed up by one of its flashiest products (Coca-Cola) while Soviet state socialism is rendered by its philosophical and political ancestors (Marx and Lenin).

ALAN WILLIAMS

2   *Pierrot* in Context(s)

It is, of course, a truism that no two people see exactly the same film, even when they see it at the same time, and in the same place. Similarly, it is by definition true that no one can see the same film (as experience) twice. For films are, to varying degrees, the products of both their particular images and sounds and of the various contexts in which they are viewed. But the degree to which this is so varies: it will be less true of "closed," stable works like *Casablanca* (Michael Curtiz, 1942) and much more so of "open," or notably "plural" works subject to multiple, often contradictory interpretations.[1] *Pierrot le fou* arguably represents an extreme example (for commercial filmmaking) of the latter category – which is another way of saying that it is a fairly representative work of the "art cinema" of its day. But *Pierrot* combines the celebrated ambiguity of the "art film" with an unusual range and quantity of cultural, intellectual, and political references.

To many viewers in the 1990s, this becomes to some extent a question of "cultural literacy": for example, Godard refers (often fleetingly) to literary figures such as Arthur Rimbaud, whose "A Season in Hell" becomes a chapter title in the film (*A-S*, 84–5, 86; *W*, 52, 56). We have to know who Rimbaud was (an outlaw poet in the great French tradition), of course, but we also want to know what Rimbaud and other such references *meant* to Godard and to the art cinema audiences (mainly students and intellectuals) of the late 1960s and early 1970s. The point cannot have been simply to show off Godard's erudition, for the cultural references are on the whole as obvious as possible: the title of Rimbaud's most famous collection of poems, of Céline's most famous novel, and so on. Godard is a bit more esoteric (but just a bit) in his cinema references; in particular, he makes offhand references to his own films that, arguably, are crucial in understanding *Pierrot le fou*. And although today we tend to think of Godard as a figure of the political left, we should remember that when the film was made a culture war was being waged *within* the left, and one of the biggest battles was over Godard himself. As we will see, *Pierrot* implicitly takes a position with respect to this frame of reference as well. One is tempted to argue that this work – which in the late 1960s and early 1970s was widely considered a profound commentary on modern society – is almost meaningless today for spectators who cannot conjure up at least some of the multiple contexts that informed its reading during the first decade or two of its career as a feature film.

MYTHS; GRIFFITH AND GODARD; THE 1960s

Jean-Luc Godard long ago entered world cinema mythology. He belongs to that very select group of directors who have been – as much as almost any celebrated actor or actress – true *stars*. His pronouncements have been repeated over and over, like his celebrated dictum that a film must have a beginning, a middle, and an end, but not necessarily in that order. He has been made to stand for whole trends or philosophies that the commentator either likes or dislikes – the "New Wave," "nonbourgeois camera style," and so on. Such is the force of his early feature work that his later films have often been criticized primarily for not measuring up to their predecessors. For like other figures of cinema myth, Godard has been perceived to set his own standards, to live in an artistic universe of his own making. *Prénom Carmen/First Name Carmen* (1983) has been seen as inferior to earlier Godard works such as *Les Carabiniers/The Soldiers* (1963) in much the same way that Hitchcock's *Topaz* (1969) is held to suffer by comparison with his great thrillers of the 1950s. At the same time, partisans of

Hitchcock or Godard can also argue that a "bad" film by their hero is better than a "good" one by someone else, which is another consequence of the separate universe inhabited by the mythic cinema artist.

But, for a time at least, Godard's status as auteur was generally perceived as more *heroic* than that of Hitchcock or any other "commercial" director.[2] The only filmmaker of greater mythic potency was probably D. W. Griffith, who until quite recently was given credit for modern narrative cinema itself, whereas Godard was seen, also until recently, as creating more or less singlehandedly an alternative ("countercinema" and the like) to it. At one point in the early 1970s, a standard film course on American university campuses was "Griffith and Godard."

All that is mostly in the past now. Griffith is no longer taught as the heroic creator of a new art form, and Godard's great early works are often relegated to the status of a curious footnote to a curious interregnum period – the 1960s. ("Interrevolutionary" would perhaps be a better word, if it existed: the decade begins in the aftermath of one failed seizure of power – by the extreme right – and ends with a similar failure on the left.) *Pierrot le fou* is one of the two or three most obviously "1960s" films by Godard; arguably, only *Week-end* (1967) exceeds it in visible marks of the period. *Pierrot* shares with *Week-end* an unusually affectionate (for Godard) attention to Nature with a capital N; a corresponding, and violent, rejection of contemporary consumer culture; a playful metacinematic texture (characters talk to the camera, and so on); significant references to contemporary political events (most notably, the war in Vietnam); and a use of color that, in the period, would qualify as "psychedelic." The director said in an interview that making *Pierrot* had been "a kind of happening" (N&M, 218; B, 265), which is to invoke one of the quintessential 1960s phenomena.

But in point of fact, *all* of Godard's early features are grounded in contemporary social reality to a degree unusual even for their period, which – we should recall – made a kind of religion of "relevance." This aspect of Godard's work, we should note, has *decreased* over time; like Jean Renoir, he moved from an early period of work dominated by specific social references (and a remarkable openness to their immediate social circle and to French society at large), through a period of artistic exile, to conclude with works centered on myth and autobiography. In other ways, too, the French filmmaker whom Godard most resembles is Renoir. Some of the similarities are comparatively trivial: both directors loved, particularly in their early careers, the sound of French spoken with nonstandard accents – Anna Karina in *Pierrot*, Nora Gregor in *La Règle du jeu/Rules of the Game* (1939), for example. There were also, at least initially, intellectual affinities: Godard in his pre-1968 period would have almost certainly agreed with the celebrated line from *La Règle du jeu:* "everyone has his [or her] reasons [for doing things]." Most significantly, both directors pose grave difficulties for auteur criticism, for two related reasons. First, their careers fall into fairly distinct periods characterized by different subject matters and formal strategies. Second, particularly in their early work they were unusually sensitive and sympathetic (as compared to their contemporaries) to the full range of their sociopolitical environments. Renoir might well have agreed with Godard, who answered critics who accused him of inappropriately dragging politics into his stories with a revealing metaphor: "[M]aking a film is an adventure comparable to that of an army advancing through a country and living off the inhabitants. So one is led to talk about those inhabitants" (N&M, 224; B, 269).

PIERROT AND POSTWAR CINEMA

But Godard in the 1950s and 1960s seems to have had (or created) even less sense of the boundaries between himself and his intellectual and social world than Renoir did in the 1930s. It is worth remembering that one of Godard's principal patrons during his formative years was Jean Cocteau, to whom the younger filmmaker dedicated an early short subject, *Charlotte et son jules* (1959). It was Cocteau who said, "I always advise the copying of a model. It is impossible to copy exactly; new blood is always infused, and it is by that that we can judge the poet."³ Godard clearly had great sympathy for this advice, which he seems to have followed even more than Cocteau himself did, suffering comparatively little from any of Harold Bloom's celebrated "anxiety of influence."⁴ To the contrary, with the striking exception of the situationists (whom we consider later, and who might be considered the exception that proves the Bloomian rule), he positively *reveled* in multiple allusions and outright admissions of influence.

Godard's willingness to share the subjects and styles of others extended during the 1960s to the other filmmakers of his generation. Oddly enough, there was no more "typical" New Wave film artist, in terms of the traits and interests he had in common with his contemporaries. With his fellow ex–*Cahiers du cinéma* critic Jacques Rivette, for example, he shared an emphasis on process, a delight in "unfinished" works, and an interest in duration (expressed, frequently, in remarkably long takes). With Alain Resnais, the central figure of the so-called Left Bank school, Godard shared a love of mixing high and low culture, and a taste – which coexisted with his Rivettian love of long takes – for montage. With the Left Bank school in general, he shared an interest in violence, madness, the shock of the real. With François Truffaut he shared a central, obsessive subject: women (what *do* they want? what are they like?). With Claude Chabrol, he shared a love of irony, although Godard's ironies are typically harder to decipher, at times even to detect. Like Eric Rohmer, he created characters who disclose themselves in intellectual discourse, which often reveals more about them than they themselves know. With almost every filmmaker of his generation, he shared a love of quotation and a profound cinephilia.

But there is a striking difference in the way in which Godard (in the 1960s) employed such themes and techniques and the way his contemporaries did. Take what is perhaps the most universal characteristic of his generation – cinephilia (literally, "love of cinema," but the French means more: devoting a large measure of one's life and self-expression to cinema). In Truffaut's *Tirez sur le pianiste/ Shoot the Piano Player* (1960), for example, a music box movement in a cigarette lighter just happens to play the main theme from Max Ophuls's *Lola Montès* (1955). But the viewer who does not know this – presumably the majority, for *Lola Montès* was the big commercial failure of the 1950s – can still understand the scene in which this *hommage* to Ophuls occurs, for it is an incidental detail in a moment of ample suspense and narrative momentum. Or, in Chabrol's *La Femme infidèle/The Unfaithful Wife* (1968), a nice bourgeois man murders his wife's lover and then cleans up the scene of the crime in a manner very reminiscent of *Psycho* (1960). But the viewer who has not seen Hitchcock's film, or who does not notice the similarities, will have no trouble understanding that the cleanup is ironically funny, and revealing of character, precisely as an expression of the man's rather prissy upper-middle-classness.

Godard's cinephilia is quite different. His references to other films and filmmakers are rarely subordinate to narrative, as virtually all details are in "classical" narrative cinema. In *Une Femme est une femme/A Woman Is a Woman* (1961), the character played by Anna Karina says – to everyone, including the film's spectators – that she would like to be in a Stanley Donan musical. This little outburst of cinephilia utterly dominates, for a moment, the progress of the film. It is thematically important (her life is too messy, and she cannot sing well enough – for MGM and Stanley Donan), but completely independent of the film's central narrative (she wants a child). Or, in *Pierrot le fou*, the great American master of low-budget (men's) genre pictures, Sam Fuller, makes an appearance at the surprise party given at Monsieur and Madame Espresso's (*A-S*, 75; W, 28–9).

This scene is terribly important for the narrative: it provides the only justification we get for why Ferdinand would want to abandon his life and family in Paris and go on the road with a woman he had an affair with more than five years before. But Fuller has nothing to do with this, narratively. Instead, he serves as thematic contrast to the partygoers (making binary opposites is one of Godard's favorite textual games). They repeat commercial slogans while he engages in dialogue; they place themselves, with little if any feeling, in relation to models from the reigning consumer culture while he speaks with self-awareness of film as a "battleground." And so on. Ultimately, the opposition within this scene is between cinema as defined and practiced by Fuller, who was a relatively individualistic, marginal filmmaker, and consumer culture.[5]

OUTLAWS AND INTELLECTUALS

Considered outside the context of the party scene, Fuller enters in other ways into the film's textual web. As the film proceeds, it spins off a series of binary oppositions, leaving it to the spectator to decide how – and if – they are connected. Fuller speaks English in the party scene, and this and his nationality connect him to the American sailor who approves, much later in the film, of Ferdinand and Marianne's skit about Vietnam (*A-S*, 92; *W*, 71). More: Fuller had himself made a film about Vietnam, *China Gate* (1957) – banned by the French government, essentially, for its anti-French view of colonial history. However, Fuller's most significant textual function in *Pierrot* is as stand-in for the types of films he made. Fuller's action dramas, such as *House of Bamboo* (1955) and *Forty Guns* (1957) – both extravagantly praised by Godard in the pages of *Cahiers du cinéma* – offer the sort of violent, individualistic narratives that Marianne says she wants to live. And in this context, Fuller enters into Godard's central dialectic – the philosophical, moral, and aesthetic conflict between his two main characters.

These two beings, in fact, want to be in two different sorts of art works. Marianne wants to live a crime drama, a film noir in fact (with herself as the femme fatale). Ferdinand wants to be in a minimalist, modernist narrative (it is he who speaks to the film audience and initiates other Brechtian gestures of self-reflexivity). To place them in the broadest categories that emerge from the director's first period, she is an outlaw, while he is an intellectual. The conflicts between their worldviews form the main textual system of the film; at times the narrative all but disappears while the couple argues or acts out disagreements in other ways. Their conflict even extends to the level of names – each character has two of them. Marianne calls her lover Pierrot, to which he almost always replies, "My name is Ferdinand." Why does she not like his given name? One reason might be that it is the name of a famous cowardly bull in children's literature. In any event, she repeatedly renames him, but he resists. Then she tries another tactic: giving his name another association, through a book by an author "with your name" – Louis-Ferdinand Céline (*A-S*, 89; cf. W, 60). But Céline, not at all coincidently, was a notorious right-wing modernist whose politics were similar to (although more extreme than) Sam Fuller's, and who told stories of lonely outsiders making a "journey to the end of the night."

The conflict of names in Marianne's case is less obvious. Her full name (or is it? – we have only Ferdinand's word for it) is only spoken twice, *off*, at the beginning and end of their first real scene together. The second time, Marianne's image is juxtaposed with that of Renoir's *Portrait of a Little Girl:* "Marianne . . . (pause, image of the painting) . . . Renoir" (*A-S*, 78; W, 34). Now Marianne has a much more celebrated reference: here there is virtually no doubt, for her name conjures up *the* Marianne, the mythical and oft-depicted Spirit of Liberty of the French Revolution.[6] This part of her name signifies the revolutionary outlaw. But Ferdinand wants to see her as a Renoir model, the object of contemplation of an artist-intellectual.

This pairing of a (revolutionary) outlaw and a (cowardly) intellectual is anything but unique in Godard's work. In fact, he started his career as a feature filmmaker with such a couple. Indeed, probably the most illuminating context for a reading of *Pierrot le fou* is its relations with the other Godard film that is, in a sense, its double: *A bout de souffle/Breathless* (1960). The following dialogue occurs when Pierrot/Ferdinand and Marianne first take to the road:

FERDINAND: It must be four years [since we saw each other].
MARIANNE: No, five and a half. It was October. (*A-S*, 76; W, 35)

Now this functions, to the spectator familiar with Godard's career (and there were many such spectators during the 1960s, although

"Marianne" from Abel Gance's *Napoleon*

far fewer today), as a clear reference to *A bout de souffle.* Beginning precisely in October 1959, five and a half years before the shooting of *Pierrot le fou,* Belmondo was playing the first of Godard's outlaws in *A bout de souffle,* opposite Jean Seberg, who played the first of his intellectuals.[7]

This is not the only echo of *A bout de souffle* in *Pierrot,* however. That the two films are intended, in a way, to function as two halves of a larger work is suggested by the fact that the first line of dialogue in *A bout de souffle,* spoken by Belmondo, begins *Après tout, je suis con,* and the last line *of Pierrot le fou* begins *Après tout, je suis idiot* (both translate as "when you get down to it, I'm really stupid"). Other details echo from film to film. For example, in Patricia's apartment in *A bout de souffle* there are reproductions of works by Renoir and Picasso; the same artists dominate the scene in the (very different) apartment where Marianne has been living at the beginning of *Pierrot.* Finally, consider names. Patricia and

Michel, *Pierrot* and *Marianne*: the initials are the same, only the sexes are reversed – and the roles of outlaw and intellectual.[8]

If we broaden the context beyond *A bout de souffle* and *Pierrot,* we can generalize a bit outside of these specific roles, although they characterize many of Godard's early works. What the outlaws and intellectuals have in common in Godard's early films is a massive dislike of, or at least indifference to, modern consumer culture. This was, to be sure, a widespread attitude during the 1960s, at least among people on the margins of French society (and specifically, among university students). But in Godard this attitude assumes a particular shape. One might specify the various possibilities open to his characters by saying that they are more or less *bored* and have more or less *courage.* Godard assumes, with the situationists and others opposed to the postwar status quo, that modern life is dehumanizing and alienated. The main result of this, for characters who have any degree at all of self-consciousness, is boredom. *L'ennui* is perhaps the principal variable that distinguishes his characters; in particular, the women may be bored to a greater or lesser degree. Marianne is easily bored, for example; Nana in *Vivre sa vie/My Life to Live* (1962) is less so. But for those whose self-consciousness pushes them to intolerable levels of ennui, the question is posed: what to do? And here emerges the second great variable: courage or the lack of it. The big switch from *A bout de souffle* to *Pierrot* is the gender reversal of this opposition. In the earlier film, it is the man who is courageous – who can "live dangerously to the very end" *[vivre dangereusement jusqu'au bout]* as a poster for a Jeff Chandler film reads. Patricia, in contrast, is not as courageous – Michel calls her *lâche,* a coward. In *Pierrot,* however, Ferdinand is the coward (in this sentence we must give him his coward's name), and Marianne the courageous one.

SITUATIONISM

That Karina's character is courageous almost goes without saying. Godard's naming her Marianne amounts to labeling her a revolutionary, in a period when there were many, at least aspiring,

Jean Seberg in *Breathless*

revolutionaries. But we can give her a more precise name, if we search the intellectual and political context of France in the 1950s and 1960s. She is a proto-situationist.

This period is far too recent for any scholarly consensus on the dominant strands in its intellectual history. Nonetheless, it seems highly likely that as a "standard account" of the 1950s and 1960s emerges, the situationists and their predecessors, the lettrists (here, it is simplest to write as if the former term includes the latter), will be crucially important. The situationists either helped organize the revolutionary energies that erupted in the "events" of May 1968, or at the very least their activities and writings *reflected* these energies. Many of the graffiti spray-painted on walls just before and during the "events" were actually citations from situationist or lettrist tracts, such as "boredom is counter-revolutionary," "take your desires for realities," or "take joy without hindrances."[9]

The situationists saw themselves as the intellectual and political heirs of Karl Marx – although they were opposed to the doctrines of postwar Marxists, who (they maintained) did not understand that society had reached a new stage of development, a stage requiring new explanations and new techniques of opposition. As Guy Debord explained it in 1967 in *The Society of the Spectacle,* previously all things had been reified as commodities; now they were further transformed into *spectacle:*

> Everything that was once directly lived has mutated into a representation. . . . The spectacle appears simultaneously as all of society, as a part of it, and as a means of its unification. . . . [At the highest level, spectacle] is not a collection *of* images; rather it is the social relations between people, mediated *by* images.[10]

With the transformation of all of society into spectacle, an authentic, satisfying life becomes virtually impossible without drastic countermeasures against the ubiquitous, poisonous illusion. Even knowing our own desires is problematic because desires have been suggested to us, as part of our roles in the spectacle. No area of culture, and certainly not Art with a capital A, is exempt from functioning within, and supporting, the system. Poetry is no better than television. "Avant-garde" artists such as the angry young men in England, or the beat writers in the United States, were deluding themselves if they thought they were doing anything besides providing the frosting on a particularly toxic cake. Art would no longer do; it was necessary to create *situations,* or proto-revolutionary adventures – opportunities for real desires, real feelings to manifest themselves. Before any better world can come into being, we have to know what we want it to be. But that is precisely what is obscured by the spectacular nature of modern consumer society; leisure time is merely time to be even more oppressed than one is at work.

One way of creating such situations was by disrupting selected public events. The lettrists broke up an Easter Sunday service at Notre Dame in 1950, and a Charlie Chaplin press conference in Paris in 1952. They were pioneers in the art of seizing the attention of the modern media apparatus for their own purposes. The demonstrations and sit-ins that characterized May 1968 had their clear predecessors in such interventions. And if such tactics were worth far more than any art work, it was still possible to create works of *anti*art. These agitators were, for example, masters of revolutionary maxims, which often appeared in Paris and elsewhere as graffiti. And they specialized in a striking way of using the dominant culture against itself, which they called *détournement*.

Détournement literally translates as "diversion" (of water) "embezzlement" (of funds), or "hijacking" (a plane); the situationist use of the term might best be rendered as "cultural highjacking," or "intellectual reappropriation." It is the modern, politicized descendant of Marcel Duchamp's technique of the found object. It consists of taking a bit of the dominant, enemy culture out of its context and redirecting its energies against the oppression of modern life (to which it originally contributed). Favored objects of *détournement* included comic strips (which could be reappropriated by giving them new captions) and advertisements (which could be manipulated in a variety of ways).

The "situs" were not alone in using such techniques of quotation and recontextualization, of course. They may be considered among the first (but not the only) radical postmodernists. As a result, the question of their influence on a filmmaker like Godard inevitably remains rather hazy and difficult. Nonetheless, they are much closer to some of his characteristic techniques than is Bertolt Brecht, whose influence is more often cited by critics. For example, Brecht remained loftily aloof from advertising campaigns, such as those Godard quotes in the party at the Espressos.

But such texts were meat and drink to the situs, who would often take images from advertising and write new texts for them. Godard does the reverse: he takes "found" advertising texts and puts them in the context of new images. This includes the ironic visual context of images dominated by red, white, or blue – not just the colors of the French flag, but of the United States as well. Such, the film seems to imply – ironically – is true patriotism.

Another bit of *détournement,* closer formally to situationist practice than the party sequence, is Godard's emphasis of the letters SS in the gasoline brand name ESSO (fascism is a type of gas) (*A-S,* 92; W, 71). Or the VIE in a neon sign that says RIVIERA (*A-S,* 85, 86; W, 54, 56). Perhaps most strikingly, there is the repeated appearance of another gasoline brand, TOTAL (*A-S,* 80, 85; W, 45, 52), which doubtless not only refers to the great power of international conglomerates, but also functions as a philosophical reference – to the idea of totality (and to the all-pervasive nature of consumer society).

THE SITUS VERSUS BRECHT; GODARD THE BOURGEOIS

Because he was an intellectual omnivore, referring constantly to all aspects of the culture of his day, Godard's pointed refusal to cite directly the work of the situationists is quite striking. Striking, but not entirely surprising: they were, as we will see, uniformly and vehemently hostile to his films. That he would have known of their activities, beginning when they were still called lettrists, is certain. The lettrists, as one of their *situations,* disrupted the Cannes film festival in 1951, demanding projection of Isidore Isou's unremittingly experimental film *Traité de bave et d'éternité* (1951). They succeeded, and a self-appointed jury headed by Jean Cocteau obtained for the work a specially created "Avant-garde Spectator's Prize." That Cocteau could be patron both to the lettrists and to *Cahiers du cinéma* critics such as Godard was a tribute to the old poet's flexibility, for the two groups roundly disliked each other. Only a year after the Cannes *manifestation,* Éric Rohmer, writing in a very early issue of the magazine, denounced Isou's work as not "serious."[11]

But if Godard never cited the lettrists/situationists, he never tired of citing some of their favorite authors. These include – in addition to the anonymous copywriters of major ad campaigns – Apollinaire, Joyce, and particularly the revolutionary orator and politician Saint-Just (the situs were the most visible group on the French left that took the Revolution, and even the Terror, as an exemplary precedent). He also quotes repeatedly from another favorite situationist text, the French *code civil* (legal code). But Godard did not name or quote the situationists themselves, even though he obviously found the revolutionary impulse of the 1960s to be of great interest. He invented a weird, fantastic band of beatnik revolutionaries for *Week-end,* and told the story of an only slightly more plausible group of Maoist terrorists in *La Chinoise* (1967), but nowhere did he directly refer to Debord, Isou, or Vaneigtem (much less to the situs in England, Switzerland, or other countries).

The most obvious explanations are often the best: Godard probably did not acknowledge the situs' existence for the very good reason that they hated him, and never tired of denouncing him and his films. For Godard was still trying to make Art, and the situs had decided that Art was the enemy. But their emnity went beyond this: it is almost certainly not a coincidence that they most hated, and denounced, two films: *A bout de souffle* and *Pierrot le fou.* For in these films, Godard came close (but not close enough!) to expounding their ideas – which made them accuse him of intellectual theft and bad faith:

> Godard is to film what Lefebvre or Morin is to social critique: each has the *appearance* of a certain freedom in style or subject matter (in Godard's case, a somewhat free manner in comparison with the stale formulas of filmic narration). But *even this freedom, they have taken from elsewhere* – from what they have managed to understand of the advanced experiences of our time. *They are the Club Med of modern thought.*[12]

The situationists saw Godard as a gutless aesthete, borrowing from others' clearer and more courageous thoughts and practices. They thought he stole their ideas, only to dilute them. But Godard did not so much dilute them, typically, as set them in opposition to a different, although also revolutionary, set of ideas and formal practices. Godard cited the work of Bertolt Brecht, and borrowed from him fairly often in these films of the 1960s (although less so afterward). A fictional Brecht takes a walk in the country in *Weekend*. In *Le Mépris/Contempt* (1963), a very real Fritz Lang talks to a character played by Brigitte Bardot of "our B. B." – and he means Brecht, not Bardot (who was famously known as B. B.). Formally, there are the chapter headings that summarize the action to come in *Vivre sa vie,* that recall Brecht's use of plot summaries as scene beginnings in plays like *Galileo* (1938/43). And, as I have already explained, in *Pierrot* (as elsewhere), Godard has a character directly address the audience.

But we should not overemphasize the presence of Brecht's theatrical techniques in Godard's early work. Not everything that "estranges" an audience is by definition Brechtian. And many aspects of Brecht's epic theater have little or no presence in Godard's films.[13] In fact, the Brechtian references and techniques may also, and perhaps more importantly, function as a way of referring to central Brechtian *ideas,* and most crucially for *Pierrot* and *A bout de souffle* the thesis – seen most clearly in *Galileo* – that there are times when being a coward is the right thing to do (however painful it can be).

All things considered, as B. B. might say, it is better to be a coward (to tell the inquisitors that the earth is really the center of the universe, to tell oneself that Marianne was all wrong and deserved to die). It is better to be Patricia in *A bout de souffle,* or an undeluded Ferdinand in *Pierrot.* Too much cowardice, though, and you are a partygoer at the Espressos. Too much courage, and you're a mass murderer or a cannibal, like the revolutionaries in *La Chinoise* and *Week-end.* As the alternatives emerge in Godard (although not in Brecht), the ideal standard is that middle ground so dear to the bourgeoisie in modern France, the *juste milieu.* But Godard is a bourgeois with a difference, for the *juste milieu* implied in works like *Pierrot le fou* is painful and unachievable. One is always tilting off in one direction or the other, or being pulled. The extremes are

Situationist comic. From Christopher Gray, *Leaving the 20th Century* (Free Fall Publications, 1974).

more easily occupied. If Godard in the 1960s is, as the situationists proclaimed, an unredeemable bourgeois, he is at least a postmodern bourgeois, full of nostalgia for a mythical middle that he can only imagine, and never find.

Godard's status as exemplary, avant-garde bourgeois also helps explain his approach to film form and style. Chopping things up and reassembling them in another order, or quoting them out of context, or citing only fragments of things, are all ways of making them beautiful. In the terms of the Russian formalists, Godard *defamiliarizes* life and cinema. But such techniques also represent a compromise: the cinematic coward would make conventional commercial narratives; the truly brave filmmaker would make either no work at all, or rejectionist ones like those produced by Isou and Debord. Godard goes for the middle. But then the problem is that the film's very beauty undermines its message. It is hard for some young viewers in the 1990s to see *Pierrot* as a film that rejects modern, spectacular, consumerist society, and this difficulty is easy enough to explain.[14] If in Godard's films the world is a nasty place where people either kill each other, or knuckle under to consumerism, the big problem in conveying this message is that the film itself is a very seductive consumer item. The cliché of bourgeois art in the nineteenth century was that it denounced the bourgeoisie; the corresponding gesture in the late twentieth century is to make a beautiful consumer good that denounces consumerism.[15]

But is this, in fact, a fatal flaw? For the politically committed viewer – and most of Godard's admirers, past and present, have been such – this boils down to another question: was the 1960s a revolutionary (or potentially revolutionary) period? If so, then Godard was presumably wrong, and the situs were right about works like *Pierrot le fou*. In the aftermath of May 1968, Godard seems to have agreed with them; he took their criticisms very much to heart, and gave himself over to support of the revolution to come. Films like *Vent d'est/Wind from the East* (1969) were much closer to situationist ideals and principles than were his earlier works. They also mystified spectators who had loved his first films and either did not like the new ones, or could not even see them in the local art house or *ciné-club*. But if the 1960s was *not* an authentically revolutionary period, then Godard's position in history changes. In a counterrevolutionary period, perhaps art works like Godard's early films are the best one can do. The situationists, after all, are almost forgotten; Godard's early films remain, to puzzle, intrigue, and delight filmgoers – and perhaps to make them think about life under late capitalism, and about their place in it.

NOTES

1. "Plural" seems to me a far more useful and precise term than "open," particularly for texts like *Pierrot le fou*. It is less awkward to speak of texts as more or less plural, as opposed to more or less "open." In *S/Z* (New York: Hill & Wang, 1974), Roland Barthes distinguishes between the "moderately plural," classical text and the "triumphantly [completely] plural." The latter is a synonym for the *writerly*, a Barthesian category that assuredly does *not* apply to the film – nor to any other specific text except "very rarely: by accident, fleetingly, obliquely in certain limit-works" (4–5). *Pierrot* would seem to fall somewhere between the two – hence the (invented) category of "notably plural."
2. The back jacket copy of Jean Collet's *Jean-Luc Godard* (New York: Crown, 1970) states unequivocally, "for better or worse, Godard is the voice of our time." Such pronouncements were far from uncommon during the 1960s and early 1970s.
3. Jean Cocteau, publicity notes for his film *Orphée/Orpheus* (1950), cited in Francis Steegmuller, *Cocteau: A Biography* (2d ed.) (Boston: Godine, 1986), 483.
4. Cf. Harold Bloom, *The Anxiety of Influence: A Theory of Poetry* (New York: Oxford University Press, 1973).
5. Fuller was always a more important film artist for French *cinéphiles* than for American ones. For one hint of his surprisingly strong influence, compare the opening sequence of his *Pickup on South Street* (1953) to the remarkably similar scene in Robert Bresson's *Pickpocket* (1959). *Hommage* is too weak a word here; "extended quotation" would be nearer the truth. (The film was initially banned in France for its anticommunism, but French *cinéphiles* saw it at the Venice festival, where it won the top award from, ironically, a left-dominated jury.)
6. Marianne may be seen leading the people to victory in countless engravings and paintings, such as Delacroix's *Liberty Leading the People* (1830). In one of her rare appearances in French cinema, she is superimposed over the concluding images of the "double tempest" sequence in Abel Gance's *Napoléon vu par Abel Gance/Napoleon* (1927).
7. Godard originally thought of his first feature film as a kind of sequel to Otto Preminger's *Bonjour Tristesse* (1958) in terms of the character played by Jean Seberg: "I could have taken the last shot of Preminger's film and started after dissolving to a title, 'Three Years

Later'" ("Interview with Jean-Luc Godard," N&M, 173; B, 218). *Pierrot le fou*, in a very real sense, has the same relation to *A bout de souffle* that that film had to Preminger's work. As if to emphasize this complicated web of connections, Godard has Seberg make a brief appearance in *Pierrot*, in footage from a film directed by her husband (of the period), Romain Gary – watched by Anna Karina, in a film directed by the latter's husband (*A-S*, 98; W, 83–4).

8. The role reversal begins at the very end of *A bout de souffle*, when Patricia appropriates Michel's Bogart-like gesture of rubbing his lip with his thumb. Note that the parallel of initials does not work if we call Belmondo's later character Ferdinand. It is Marianne who wants to be in a rewrite of *A bout de souffle;* presumably her lover does not.

9. The latter catch phrase, in French *jouissez sans entraves*, is almost impossible to translate: *jouir* means both "to enjoy" and "to have an orgasm." The phrase is from a book by the situationist Raoul Vaneigtem, *Traité de savoir-vivre à l'usage des jeunes générations* (Paris: Gallimard, 1967) and can be seen in a celebrated photo by Cartier-Bresson taken in May 1968. This and other facts in this section may be found in Kevin LaMastra, "En cherchant une image de Godard dans la Société du Spectacle" (New Brunswick, NJ: Rutgers University, unpublished senior honors thesis, 1992).

10. Guy Debord, *The Society of the Spectacle,* Chapter 1, paragraphs 1, 3, and 4. Multiple versions are available: I have based this brief free rendering (emphasis is my own) on the second edition of the translation from Black and Red (Detroit, 1977).

11. Maurice Schérer [Éric Rohmer], "Isou, ou les choses telles qu'elles sont," *Cahiers du cinéma* 2, 10 (1952): 27–32.

12. Anon., "Le Rôle de Godard," *Internationale situationniste* 10 (1966), translated in Ken Knabb (ed. & trans.), *Situationist International Anthology* (Berkeley: Bureau of Public Secrets, 1981), 176. The translation has been slightly modified, and the last emphasis added by the present author. (This collection includes a number of other commentaries on Godard.)

13. See Roland Barthes's comments on the "social gesture" in "Brecht, Eisenstein, Diderot," in Stephen Heath (ed. & trans.), *Image, Music, Text* (New York: Hill & Wang, 1977), 69–78. In the terms of Barthes's argument, Eisenstein is far more Brechtian than early Godard.

14. I base this comment on my experience teaching the film in undergraduate film classes – almost the only context in which it is regularly screened these days. My students are mostly middle class, from a variety of national and racial backgrounds; the film mystifies all but a small minority. A first question is almost always, "Why does Pierrot want to leave Paris?"

15. The feature films of Godard's third period – which begins with

Sauve qui peut (la vie)/Every Man for Himself (1979) and includes such films as *Prénom Carmen* – do not suffer from this contradiction. They are more austere and less obviously beautiful than those of the 1960s; they are wiser, arguably more profound works, but they have not inspired the fierce love (and hate) that his films of the 1960s once did. In my view this is, precisely, because they are so much less seductive – at least on first viewing.

3 Godard's Tricolor

POSTCARDS AND FRESCOES

Jean-Luc Godard calls *Pierrot le fou* the antithesis of Luchino Visconti's *Senso* (1954). All of the moments that he would have wanted to see in *Senso* (a film that in other respects he "likes") are precisely those that Visconti does not show.[1] A declaration such as that, concerning the means of narration, holds as well for references on the pictorial level; *Pierrot le fou* is not a "historical" film. It is normal, as in *Senso,* for Countess Livia and her lover to move through mansions adorned with frescoes, rubbing shoulders with their characters with the easy familiarity of those who have behind them centuries of accumulated history. Pierrot-Ferdinand, in contrast, moves instead through the *Histoire de l'art* by Élie Faure in a pocket edition, and frequents art works in the form of postcards that one can tack to the wall. His experience is that of the ordinary twentieth-century person who approaches art through commentaries and reproductions.

Senso always keeps its actors in the same proportions as its frescoes: not only are the *real* frescoes filmed but they are filmed in their exact dimensions, that is, to human measure, since they serve as the frame for life itself. The film shows Alida Valli and Farley Granger either in front of or beside them. In *Pierrot le fou,* the

This essay is extracted from Jean-Louis Leutrat, *Kaléidoscope* (Lyon: Presses Universitaires de Lyon, 1988), 85–111, and reprinted with permission. All notes are translators' notes and all translations from French sources are ours.

works either take up the whole screen or they are small-scale reproductions that are at times difficult to see beside the actors. The
result is that the Visconti film characters Countess Livia Serpieri
and Lieutenant Franz Mahler are always distinguishable when associated with the characters in the frescoes; the trompe l'œil must
always appear as such in order to suggest the contrived and illusory
character of the countess's passion (as for Franz Mahler's passion,
Farley Granger's acting suffices to show its falseness).

On the other hand, Godard postulates an identity between his
characters and the representations that accompany them. For
example, Marianne and Auguste Renoir's woman coincide to the
extent that the character is named Marianne Renoir. After the
famous "lovers of the night" scene that ends (on the sound track)
with the song *C'que t'es belle, ma pépé, c'que t'es belle, c'que t'es belle*
["How beautiful you are my little one"], there appears a wide-
angle shot of Marianne in her apartment saying, "We'll see" *[On
verra bien]* (A-S, 78; W, 37). Ferdinand's voice then sets the
"equals" sign between Marianne and Renoir, establishing a bridge
between them and the next shot, the face of Renoir's *La Petite fille
à la gerbe* (1888) (Marianne as child-woman with a red ribbon in
her hair). A little further, Marianne leaning against a wall is juxtaposed with a *Baigneuse* from 1880, the face of which is used again
a short while later (in *A bout de souffle*, Patricia invites comparison
with the portrait of *Mlle. Irène Cahen d'Anvers*, also from 1880). In
terms of the enunciation, these two paintings do not have the
same status; one *(La Baigneuse)* belongs to the diegetic universe,
and the other *(La Petite fille à la gerbe)* does not, but both belong to
a Renoir series that is completed at another moment of the film
with a *Nude* seen from behind, lying down, between two shots of
sparkling sea ("he told them about the summer, and the desire
that lovers have to breathe the cool evening air" [A-S, 84; W, 49]).

As *A bout de souffle* allows us to predict, the Renoir series inter-
sects with one by Picasso. In the scene that takes place in her
apartment, Marianne does her hair in front of a mirror: *Jeune
femme au miroir* from 1932 is pinned to the wall. Picasso also
serves as an allusion to Pierrot-Ferdinand: above the bed he is

lying in we see *Paul en Pierrot* (1925). In another passage of the film, the one where Marianne stabs the short man in the neck with a pair of scissors, two 1954 Picasso paintings are shown hanging on the wall (*Jacqueline aux fleurs* and *Sylvette au fauteuil vert*) (*A-S*, 94–6; W, 77–8). At some point between these two scenes *Les Amoureux* from 1923 is shown as we hear the words "Tender is the night. . . . It was a love story" (*A-S*, 80; W, 46) (and when this same *Amoureux* appears seen with *Jacqueline aux fleurs* in Patricia's apartment in *A bout de souffle,* Patricia says, "I wish we were Romeo and Juliet").

Thus two important series are connected with painting and they are represented principally in two scenes where a man has been killed by Marianne with a pair of scissors, evoking *Dial M for Murder* (Alfred Hitchcock, 1954) (M as in Marianne). The Picasso series insists on duplicity and disguise (already a theme of *A bout de souffle* and given emphasis in *Pierrot le fou* with the text that states, "We have entered the age of the Double-Man" [*A-S*, 93; W, 74]). *Paul en Pierrot* (there are two of them) recalls Pierrot-Ferdinand; the double face of the *Jeune femme au miroir* recalls that of Marianne, echoing both Renoir (Marianne = *aimer Anna* [love Anna]), and Modigliani. The latter's *Lady with a Black Tie* from 1917 is over the bed on which the dead body lies in Marianne's apartment.

In the second scene, Marianne appears between *Jacqueline aux fleurs* and *Portrait de Sylvette;* in a neighboring room two photographs of naked women echo this double representation, one woman exhibiting herself, the other chained in a sadistic scene. These series can either interconnect or constitute relatively autonomous compositions. During the passage in Marianne's apartment (*A-S*, 78; W, 40), she moves from room to room singing a song about the precariousness of the love "with no tomorrow" that she and Ferdinand are embarked upon. Then the camera cuts to a close-up of her saying, "We'll see," while on the sound track a piano plays *Au clair de la lune, mon ami Pierrot* across four shots that emphasize the role played by painting: *Paul en Pierrot* (in close-up), the 1940 *Blouse roumaine* by Matisse, *Paul en Pierrot* (in extreme close-up), and the face of the *Baigneuse* from 1880. On

Marianne, Picasso, and the short man

the sound track, Marianne and Ferdinand converse (Ferdinand speaking over a picture of a woman and Marianne speaking over one of a man). Marianne tells Ferdinand that his wife has been there. *La Blouse roumaine* might thus allude to Ferdinand's wife, and this series of four shots can be read as a "metaphorical" representation of Ferdinand's situation as he chooses between two women. The painted figures easily take the place of the characters, and the latter continuously comment on each other's actions, as if each were the narrator of the other's story. Again a series seems to be formed.

In the apartment where the short man dies, two Picassos on the wall form a "composition." One shot shows Marianne holding her arm extended while, with a *pair* of scissors that she opens and closes, she moves her arm from right to left (*A-S*, 96; *W*, 79). The hand holding the scissors in the first shot has the same dimensions as the face that stands out in the background between

Jacqueline aux fleurs (on the right) and *Portrait de Sylvette* (on the left), these two works of Picasso being in profile, turned to the left. The first of these paintings is divided into two parts: the upper part is blue and the other red; they are separated by a diagonal as if the painter had juxtaposed two pieces of paper previously cut with scissors (an instrument that, as we know, reminds us of the editing process. M[arguerite] Renoir was a famous editor.). In the painting the model's neck is noticeably elongated, a deformity that finds an equivalent in the treatment of the shot, filmed in tight focus. Several shots later, Ferdinand occupies the same position as Marianne on the screen, but he turns slightly to the right (in profile then, like the painted figures, but in the opposite direction and not full frontal as was Marianne). He is about to be beaten up by one of the thugs. The violence of the scene is not shown, no more than was the murder of the little man; only on the sound track do we hear several cries of pain. *Jacqueline aux fleurs* is in close up, right side up, then reversed, upside down. These two shots are followed by one of the *Portrait de Sylvette*, also in close-up (*A-S*, 96; *W*, 80). The portraits certainly do not remind us of Pierrot-Ferdinand; at the outside they might bring Marianne to mind. It seems to be their color that counts most here. In fact the framing of the shot allows us to see only the blue section of *Jacqueline aux fleurs*. All three shots emphasize this color. Red, however, is linked to Marianne (she wears a red dress) and to the murder she commits ("not blood, red"[2]). When Ferdinand enters the room with the white walls where the short man's body lies, the red of a chair, a round cushion, the dress Marianne has left behind, and a lamp shade (as in the apartment in *Une Femme est une femme/A Woman Is a Woman* [1961]), stands out against the white. And the red of the blood has spilled onto a white carpet, evoking the Japanese flag, while a blue ashtray announces the imminent "beating" *[passage à tabac]*. If red is blood, then blue represents the blows, the color of bruises.[3] Everything can be turned around, however; Ferdinand's torturers cover his face with the red dress (associated therefore with blows), and at the end of the film, Ferdinand paints his face blue (death).

The painting-film cut up

Godard's attention to the blue, white, and red, which runs through all of his work, relates him closely to the Fauves, for whom the populist flag-waving of July 14 became an emblem (Marquet, Dufy, Manguin, and before them, Manet, Monet, van Gogh). Like them, Godard treats color in pure, saturated tones, privileging the flat matte surface, that is to say, the nonillusionist picture plane. The contrast with Visconti could not be greater. For the Italian director, color "is not excessive or symbolic, but dramatic: pleasure is taken in the sign, rather than work performed on the signifier. Everything is integrated and participates in the denotation."[4] Still, there are moments in *Senso* where the color oscillates between a traditional symbolic value (the red of the couch and curtains in the countess's bedroom, for example, recalls the opera and its ardor of love) and an autonomous function that makes it either proliferate or contract. In the room where Livia hands over the florins from the Italian cause to the Austrian lieutenant, the yellow that, up to this point in the sequence, has remained localized on the collar of the uniform jacket and on the piping of Franz Mahler's pants, suddenly begins to "overflow": the whole room becomes engorged with yellow like a drink that goes to your head. We can always affirm that this profusion of gold denotes a concern with harmonizing the upholstery of the chairs and the tones of the frescoes decorating the room; however, a limit is crossed, an excess committed. At this moment the two characters are beside themselves, the countess caught in a suicidal slide and Franz Mahler moved beyond anything he might have hoped for. We could speak of symbolism if this colored drunkenness were not itself glutted with signifieds: the florins, the Austrian uniform, the opera's gold, the summer harvest (whose "intoxicating" odor Franz had praised shortly before), betrayal, and so on. In another sense, color can occupy a modest but stubborn place. This is what occurs with the veil of green tulle whose (reduced) presence is even more insistent because at no moment in the film does the countess wear this color. The veil itself becomes part of a chain of signifieds, but the color green creates an acid stain that exceeds all sense.

Color in *Senso* generally responds to a logic of centering that permits us to speak of decentering in the examples just mentioned. Decentering is only perceptible through the surfeit of the presence of the center, and on various occasions it is presented as double. With Godard, the center has disappeared. There is no longer a privileged point, but there are series that affirm their differences for themselves. We can speak of off-centering or eccentricity *[excentration]*: the center is diluted into the periphery.

The Zelotti frescoes that Visconti has chosen to show are principally trompe l'œil. Pierre Charpentrat has described an *Annunciation* by Crivelli[5] as "a magnificent gradation of planes articulated by the architecture and duly confirmed by the proportions of the figures." And he adds,

> Who, moreover, would be tempted to see in these irreproachable perspectives an extension of our own world? But there in the foreground, an apple and a zucchini placed on the tiles, a tapestry

enlivened by large folds hanging from a balcony, and a peacock perching on a cornice all stand out from the painting and infringe upon the spectator's universe. We are not truly fooled, we do not hold out our hands to touch the zucchini, despite its salient position and insistent shadows, because it remains, in spite of everything, partly imprisoned within the ambient fiction. . . . The *trompe-l'œil* itself is in no way felt as an imitation, as a reflection. When it succeeds completely, it refers, precisely, to nothing but itself. If Crivelli inserts several otherwise useless objects between his *Annunciation* and us, it is an attempt to persuade us that the work constitutes something other than a simple representation, other than a reminder of a pre-existent reality. For the transparent, allusive image that awaits the art-lover, the *trompe-l'œil* tends to substitute the uncompromising opacity of a Presence.[6]

When Visconti places Alida Valli or Farley Granger (playing for the occasion the role of the apple or the zucchini) next to a trompe l'œil fresco, he is using a now vanished mode of expression that his movie, in a certain way, wants to reactivate. However, he knows that "the uncompromising opacity of a Presence" belongs to another age. There is thus a sort of defective alignment between that project and this declaration, and the decenterings derive precisely from such defective alignments.

The word *decenter* comes from the vocabulary of optics; *eccentricity* is a turner's term that fits well a cinematographer who privileges the hands over the eyes.[7] *Excentricus* means "that which is offcenter." The center is a point of view on things, but things and beings represent so many points of view. Godard says, "directing is first and foremost humbly taking the side of things *[le parti des choses].*"[8]

COLOR IN THE MARGINS

There is a place traditionally devoted to what is literally legible in the margins of film. It is the credits considered as an outgrowth of the movie. Their institutional function consists in paying tribute to each contributor according to his or her due, in the form of a "nomination." To have one's name in the credits is to be recognized in a certain manner. The size of the name differs according to the importance of the work done, or more simply according to one's draw at the box office. The credits thus constitute both an official technical record *[fiche technique]* and a program such as in a theater or concert hall. But the credits are not made up of names only. There are diverse procedures for presenting them and they have varied from one period to another and even within a single period. The credits can be conceived of as a book whose pages are turned in the way a theater curtain is opened. The names could parade across a simple background or against the backdrop of a scene that has already begun. Some credits are preceded by a sequence, and others are placed at the end of a film.

The screening of *Une Femme est une femme* begins with two credits announcing in blue, white, and red the prizes won at festivals by the film and the actress (these elements, which, of course, were added later, are integrated into the film thanks to these colors). Then, over a dark screen, we hear the sound of an orchestra conductor's baton tapping on his music stand. Twenty more credits then follow on a black background (in blue, white, and red letters). The background sound for the first credit is a voice ("Hurry . . . hurry . . . take your places"), and for the rest one hears the sounds of instruments being tuned.

ONCE UPON – white	MUSICAL – white
A TIME – white	LEGRAND – red
BEAUREGARD – red	THEATRICAL – red
EASTMANCOLOR – white	EVEIN – red
PONTI – red	SENTIMENTAL – white
FRANKLY SCOPE – white	GUILLEMOT – red
GODARD – red	OPERA – white
COMÉDIE – white	LUBITSCH – blue
FRANÇAISE – white	JULY 14TH – blue
COUTARD – red	CINEMA – red

These credits differ from traditional ones in several ways:

    1. The visual and audio elements composing them are very different. After the twenty credits, there follow three shots composed of each of the three main actors with

their names and, on the sound track, a feminine voice saying one word for each: "Lights . . . Camera . . . Action."
Finally, the film's title appears in red letters over a shot of
an empty, silent street.

2. The size of the letters in the titles. Each title carries
only a single word or a single name. All the words and
names are of the same size (nobody is "privileged").
Nowhere does a first name precede a family name. No
indication of profession is given. Only the actors receive
special treatment; their names are not on a black background, but in shots in which they are themselves shown.

3. The presence of disruptive words that do not ordinarily have a place in title sequences. Not only do these
credits not contain the information we expect from a
technical record, but the sequence presumes to give clues
as to how the film is to be read.

4. The separation of words and names by color that
underlines the striking disparity of the blue. We can count
ten elements in white, eight in red, and two in blue. The
spectator has hardly any choice but to read these credits;
the size of the letters (taking up the whole screen) forces
us to pay attention to them. And because the credits run
by at a rather fast rate, it is not possible to linger. The
spectator is thus expected to read actively and to establish
relations between one word and another. As a result, four
different procedures can be envisaged:

i) The most simple procedure consists in following
the order of the credits. "Once upon a time Beauregard"
has a sense. "Musical" links with "Legrand" (Michel,
the musician); "theatrical" with "Evein" (Bernard, the
set designer); "sentimental" with "Guillemot" (Agnès
the editor); "July 14th" with "cinema," "comédie" with
"française." One can read this as so many lighthearted
clues to the functioning of the editing and decor, and
Godard seems to say that his film should be understood
as a sort of cinematic celebration or holiday or that cinema is a holiday. The names of the producers (Georges

de Beauregard and Carlo Ponti) alternate with those of the technical processes (Eastmancolor and Franscope); those of Godard and Coutard surround "*Comédie française*"; and the words "opera" and "cinema," the name of Ernst Lubitsch and the mention "July 14th."

ii) Another way to read these credits would be to try to establish thematic links among them. *Comédie française* is associated with theatrical, *comédie* with Lubitsch and musical,[9] *française* with July 14th and Franscope (and with the three colors blue, white, and red), theatrical with opera, opera with musical, Beauregard with cinema (for what is cinema but a beautiful sight *[beau regard]?*).

iii) Links established by means of assonance take place on their own. Beauregard is associated with Godard and Coutard; theatrical with musical and sentimental; Karina rhymes with opera and cinema; Ponti with comedy and Brialy.

iv) The names and words can be read according to their groupings in relation to each of the three colors:

– Red is limited to the more traditional list of technical record. With but one exception (cinema), it is used only for family names: Beauregard, Ponti, Godard, Coutard, Legrand, Evein, and Guillemot. The word "cinema" at the end of the series assembles all of the enumerated individuals and all of the "professions" they represent.

– White indicates, in the first place, the genre from which the film arises: the fairy tale ("Once upon a time"); French as opposed to American comedy. White also designates the tone (sentimental), a kind of *mise-en-scène* (theatrical, musical, opera), the technical processes (Eastmancolor, Franscope). The director's taste for wordplay is expressed in the credit "Frankly Scope," which designates the Franscope format. We are given to understand that

certain films using the wide screen do so shame-
fully. Godard's pleasure at using the wide screen for
the first time also shines through here. Finally,
"Frankly Scope" contains "Franscope" just as the
wide screen contains the normal format.

– Blue is reserved for *(cinéphile)* cultural references;
Ernst Lubitsch and his *Design for Living* (1933) on
the one hand, and René Clair and his *14 juillet/July
14th* (1933) on the other. For variety, Godard gives
the name of a director and a film title, but he
chooses those that have a meaning for the spectator: July 14th recalls something entirely different
from a film (which is not the case for *Design for Living*), and Lubitsch is the name of the character
played by Jean-Paul Belmondo in *Une Femme est une
femme*. Godard has written that this character cherishes a vain dream just like Paula Illery does for
Albert Préjean in *July 14th* by René Clair, which he
considers to be a great film: "Here the audience real-
izes that Émile plus Angéla plus Alfred = *Sérénade à
trois*.[10] That [the Belmondo character] Alfred
Lubitsch, in other words, would like to make it with
Angéla. Very much so. But also, that, like Paula
Illery in the superb *14 juillet*, he cherishes a vain
dream" (N&M, 167, translation modified; B, 212).

These twenty credits teach us a great deal about the film. While
they follow one another in the style of a blinking electric sign
announcing an imminent spectacle (or an imminent catastrophe),
the sound track has us hear an orchestra of musicians tuning their
instruments. No doubt that accounts for the rapid rhythm of the
credits: "Hurry . . . hurry . . . take your places." The names and
words of the credits are like the musicians in the orchestra who
are going to interpret what follows. The two credits "musical" and
"opera," and the name of Michel Legrand, insist on *Une Femme est
une femme*'s relation with music. But we must not fool ourselves:
"The film is not a musical. It's the idea of a musical. . . . You have

to do something different: my film says this too. It is nostalgia for the musical."[11]

The three colors – "for me, the film also meant the discovery of color and direct sound" (N&M, 182; B, 224) – are those associated with Anna Karina's character: "Two blue eyes: Giraudoux, a red umbrella: Aragon"[12] (N&M, 166; B, 211) and the white raincoat and red stockings . . . three colors, three characters, and three actors. The two men are motionless, the woman is in motion, shot from a low angle, cut off at the waist, putting on her "theatrical" costume. Her active dimension contrasts with the waiting posture of the two men. This is reinforced by the fact that the three terms indicating that the filming is about to begin are spoken by Anna Karina:

• Light: bright, but also lightweight (Brialy is a brilliant but "light" actor).
• Camera: Karina/Camera.
• Action: No doubt this is to be understood ironically because nothing works out for Belmondo in this film.

Three terms, three shots, a woman between two men, three actors, three colors, three series, like the three knocks that start everything in the theater or in *The Most Dangerous Game* (Irving Pichel and Ernest Schoedsack, 1932).[13] The titles end with the shot during which Angéla enters. It shows a window, and through this window, a street. Cars and pedestrians pass. The red title comes to be written on the windowpane. Lipstick is put on. The shot is silent, one waits. The red of the title calls forth the red of Angéla's umbrella. The lack of characters asks to be filled, the silence to be broken: in just a moment a woman will enter the field of vision.

THE DISPOSSESSING GAZE

At the beginning of *Le Mépris/Contempt* (1963), after the appearance of "Cocinor" in blue, white, and red, then of the title in red letters on a black background (at that moment the music begins), we see a space shot with an extreme depth of field, representing an exterior with, to the right, the rails for a dolly shot and to the left, buildings. Between the two, a rather large empty space. In the background, a camera surrounded by several technicians follows laterally a woman coming toward us and reading. A boom operator holds a microphone over her. Once the camera in the shot has filled the frame (the woman has thus left the field of vision), an upward pan comes to rest on that camera in the image, seen from below. The cameraman, who has remained in the shot, turns to the sun to measure the intensity of the light, then toward the viewfinder of the camera and pivots it horizontally through a quarter turn. He then pans it downward so that the lens of the camera shooting from above looks directly into the camera filming it from below.

Instead of watching the opening credits roll over these images, we hear a sound track: continuous music (beginning strongly, emphatically, over the title) and a text spoken in monotone:[14]

It's based on the novel by Alberto Moravia. There is Brigitte Bardot and Michel Piccoli. There is also Jack Palance and Georgia Moll . . . and Fritz Lang. The cinematography is by Raoul Coutard. Georges Delerue wrote the music, and the sound was recorded by William Sivel. The editing is by Agnès Guillemot. Philippe Dusart was Production Manager, assisted by Carlos Lastricati. This is a Jean-Luc Godard film. It is shot in cinemascope and the color processing was done by G.T.C. in Joinville. It was produced by Georges de Beauregard and Carlo Ponti for the Rome-Paris Films company, and Concordia Cinematografica Champion in Rome. Cinema, says André Bazin, substitutes for our view of the world a world that accords with our desires. *Le Mépris* is the story of this world.

By having this title sequence spoken, Godard indicates that this is the text he wants the spectator to attend to. There where *Une Femme est une femme* lets us hear the preparations for a concert, then for filming, and shows giant credits, *Le Mépris* reverses the order. The credits this time pass through the ear (they are given with the film, as in *Othello*, mixed with the music) and we watch a scene being shot. At the same time as the first images appear, the film is designated in deictic terms: "It's based on the novel by . . . ," as something that is already there (the title is at the beginning of the credits, and not at the end), spoken of with a sort of respectful fear, as if it were as a sacred object.

The feminine character followed by a camera is an actress (Georgia Moll) who is playing the role of a script girl in the filming of a movie based on *The Odyssey*. Which camera is filming her? That which takes care of the filming of the film within the film? Why would it film this young woman who is not an actress? It cannot be the camera that shoots *Le Mépris*, which, by definition, cannot be represented; and yet the man behind the camera is Raoul Coutard and, several moments later when Francesca accompanies Paul who is speaking with Jeremiah, the two characters retrace, in the opposite direction, the path followed by the woman in the opening shot. This walk down a street in Cinecittá is shown by a dolly shot taken from the same position as that of the camera we see in the opening sequence. The same uncertainty applies to the female character: Francesca, Georgia Moll, or Minerva "reciting her lines" as Claude Ollier affirms.[15] Is she reciting lines from somewhere else? She apparently does not say a single word: the boom that follows her does not seem to serve any purpose and the voice we hear, which should be feminine, is masculine. On the other hand, she is reading a book: *The Odyssey? Le Mépris?* The fact that the act of reading usually carried out by the spectator at the beginning of a film is associated here with this young woman designates the dispossession that the spectator has fallen prey to, warning of a more radical dispossession to come.

Once only the camera remains in the image, we hear the words attributed to André Bazin. Godard had already quoted this sentence two years earlier in the commentary that he wrote for the record jacket of *Une Femme est une femme*. "Since, as Bazin said, the cinema usurps the role of our eyes to present a world consonant with our desires, it was extraordinarily tempting to make a Mitchell 300 usurp the gaze of this young Parisian" (N&M, 166, translation modified; B, 211). At the end of the shot-sequence which opens *Le Mépris*, it is the gaze of a camera that is visible in the image. But this look does not substitute for any other, and certainly not for that of the young woman being filmed. In *Une*

Femme est une femme, a play of relays is established between the spectator and the camera, a play in which the heroine has a central place. In *Le Mépris* there is no longer any character to perform this relay. The cinema substitutes a world in accord with our desires for our gaze (it no longer substitutes *itself* for our gaze) by setting this latter aside, by erasing it. But this conformity of world and gaze does not prevent the erasing of the subject as the source of the gaze; it does not prevent it from being "sponged." In 1950 Godard wrote, "at the cinema we do not think, we are thought. A poet calls this 'taking the side of things' *[le parti pris des choses].* Not man's view of things, but taking the side of things themselves" (N&M, 19, translation modified; B, 74). Which comes back to saying that in the cinema we are dispossessed of the powers attributed to the subject as master of what he perceives as of himself.

At the end of the shot-sequence in *Le Mépris,* when the voice falls silent, there remain the blue sky (just as, at the end of the film, there is the orange curve of the sea), and a camera pointing at us (the boom also leans in our direction). Godard wanted his film to be seen from above (Lang's "lucid gaze . . . the film's conscience, the moral link"), so "the gaze of the camera . . . replaces that of the gods,"[16] those very gods who represented a world in accord with our desires. What happens when the gods are absent? There remains the cinema, and when this last "ordeal of expression" is over, there remains the "history" of this ordeal:

> Like the sponge, the orange, after undergoing the ordeal of expression, longs to recover its composure. The sponge always succeeds, though, the orange never: for its cells have burst, its tissues are torn apart. Only the peel, thanks to its elasticity, to some extent regains its shape. Meanwhile an amber liquid has been spilled, which, refreshing and fragrant as it may be, often bears the bitter consciousness of a premature expulsion of pits.[17] (Translated by David Laatsch and David Wills)

NOTES

1. See "Let's Talk About *Pierrot,*" N&M, 222; B, 267:

> The great traditional cinema means Visconti as opposed to Fellini or Rossellini. It is a way of selecting certain scenes rather than others. The Bible is also a traditional book since it effects a choice in what it describes. If

I were ever to film the life of Christ, I would film the scenes which are left out of the Bible. In *Senso,* which I quite like, it was the scenes which Visconti concealed that I wanted to see. Each time I wanted to know what Farley Granger said to Alida Valli, bang! – a fade-out. *Pierrot le fou,* from this standpoint, is the antithesis of *Senso:* the moments you do not see in *Senso* are shown in *Pierrot.*

2. Godard's reply, in the *Cahiers du cinéma* interview, to the suggestion that there is a good deal of blood in the film. See N&M, 217; B, 264.
3. Fr. *"des bleus."*
4. Youssef Ishaghpour, *Visconti. Le sens et l'image* (Paris: Éditions de la Différence, 1984), 74.
5. Giambattista Zelotti (1526–78), Veronese school, known for fresco paintings in Veneto villas; Carlo Crivelli (c. 1430–1500), Venetian, second-generation renaissance painter.
6. Pierre Charpentrat, "Le Trompe-l'œil," *Nouvelle revue de la psychanalyse* 4 (1971): 161–2.
7. French for "shooting a film" is *tourner.*
8. Commentary by Godard for the record of *Une Femme est une femme,* N&M, 168, translation modified; B, 213.
9. French for "musical" is *comédie musicale.*
10. "Serenade for three," the French title for *Design for Living.*
11. Interview with Jean-Luc Godard. N&M, 182; B, 224.
12. Jean Giraudoux (1882–1944) and Louis Aragon (1897–1982) were important French literary figures. Angéla first appears in the film carrying a red umbrella. See *A Woman Is a Woman* in *Godard: Three Films* (New York: Harper & Row, 1975).
13. In France the beginning of a play is traditionally signaled by three knocks of a cane, just as three knocks on the door of Count Zaroff's castle begin the action in *The Most Dangerous Game.*
14. In the English version of the film, credits are indeed shown, in red, during this first tracking shot. The voice-over described here is neither heard nor translated.
15. Claude Ollier, *Souvenirs Écran* (Paris: Éditions Cahiers du Cinéma-Gallimard, 1981), 174.
16. Jean-Luc Godard, "Scénario du *Mépris,"* B, 244, 249.
17. Francis Ponge, "L'Orange" (*Le Parti pris des choses* [Paris: Éditions Gallimard, 1942]), trans. C. K. Williams, in Margaret Guiton (ed.), *Selected Poems* (Winston-Salem, NC: Wake Forest University Press, 1994), 22–5:

> Comme dans l'éponge il y a dans l'orange une aspiration à reprendre contenance après avoir subi l'épreuve de l'expression. Mais où l'éponge réussit toujours, l'orange jamais : car ses cellules ont éclaté, ses tissus se sont déchirés. Tandis que l'écorce seule se rétablit mollement sa forme grâce à son élasticité, un liquide ambre s'est répandu, accompagné de rafraîchissement, de parfum suave, certes – mais souvent aussi de la conscience amère d'une expulsion prématurée de pépins.

4 Language Gone Mad

What is it like to go mad? Since the Middle Ages the question has driven French and Francophone writers into a state of heightened frenzy. Poets and artists test the limits of language and representation by leading their work into spaces approaching alterity and nonsense. *Pierrot le fou* figures prominently in this tradition. A rich and variegated essay about the madness of cinema and the politics and aesthetic of the medium, the film aligns itself with some of the most probing literary experiments that have tested the limits of meaning. Like Godard himself, viewers who have been weaned on French literature know that every work of stature somewhere tends to go mad: it abandons its path of reason, science, intellect, and intelligence in hazarding into rich and dubious areas where, within even the strictest controls of logic and grammar, unconscious forces emanate from worlds unknown.

In French the cast of characters who let their idiom go to their heads is long. Chrétien de Troye's gallant Yvain succumbs to folly when in love. In the novel of about 1170 that bears his name, he becomes a naked beast who eats raw venison in the depths of the Brocéliande Forest. In 1532, in *Pantagruel*, Rabelais's Panurge comes to Paris in the guise of a madman or trickster who exceeds the model of wise Folly drawn from Erasmus and Pauline Scripture. Soon after, Montaigne praises the possessed souls who resist reason in "Of Cripples" (1558), an essay that has inspired the novel and film about the return of Martin Guerre. Molière's Harpagon goes berserk on stage when he loses his money box in

L'Avare (1666), a grim comedy about the madness of self-posses-
sion. In the modern world, ostensibly closer to Godard, Arthur
Rimbaud is crazed by alterity in his adolescent lyric verse before
he himself, their author, becomes *autre* ("other"). In the 1940s
Antonin Artaud ends his literary career with letters written from
an insane asylum in Rodez.

Godard's masterpiece figures in this tradition. It indicates, perhaps better than any work of the last fifty years, exactly why and
how madness is related to our most urgent and immediate con-
sciousness of the world we inhabit. But most important, it shows
how film is the very medium of language in a state of virtual madness. In what follows, at the risk of falling under the spell of *Pierrot,* I attempt to sort through three issues pertaining to the madness of the film's language. First, I recall the philosophical context
of discussions about madness in the early 1960s, the time when
Pierrot was conceived and made. Second, by means of a close reading of the opening shots and their aftereffects, I discern how a
concurrently literary and cinematic madness of vision is put forward in strange articulations of signs, words, letters, and images.
From the credits to the first time that "madness" is mentioned in
the film, in the fourth shot, we witness a revolution taking place
in the very process of the apprehension of film. The way that *Pierrot* forces us to look at film from an almost maddeningly different
perspective leads, finally, to speculation about the world at large
and the immensity of a fragmented extension concealed in every
one of its details. The ambition of this essay, then, is to map out
the way that the film folds entire *worlds* of sensation and language
in its style of composition.

FILM AND FOLLY: AN OVERVIEW

Madness is cast all over the surface of the film. Ferdinand's
wife tells the protagonist that he is "mad" to describe to their
daughter the idiotic world in which Velázquez painted dwarfs and
imbeciles (sequence 4; *A-S,* 72; W, 24).[1] Marianne, at the beginning of her fling with Ferdinand, intones that in their love they

share "such *mad* and violent feelings" [*ces sentiments si* fous *et si violents*] (sequence 9; *A-S*, 78; W, 39), feelings so heady that Ferdinand must avow he couldn't care less about the consequences of his actions: "Basically," he exclaims, "I totally don't give a damn" [*Dans le fond je m'en* fous *totalement*] (sequence 9; *A-S*, 78; cf. W, 40). Madame Ferdinand, in a flashback, utters about her husband, after he leaves his family, "I don't understand it at all. He's just gone mad" [*Il est devenu* fou] (sequence 16; *A-S*, 86, W, 54). Marianne tells Ferdinand that he is *"fou"* for having spoken to the spectator while they drive their Ford Galaxy southward (sequence 17; *A-S*, 86; W, 55). In contrast to Ferdinand's interest in books Marianne quips, "I couldn't care less" [*Je m'en fiche*] (sequence 27; *A-S*, 93; W, 72). The singer Raymond Devos implores Ferdinand to tell him he is mad [*Dites que je suis* fou!], to whom Ferdinand dutifully responds, *"vous êtes* fou" (sequence 50; *A-S*, 106; W, 101). When an image of a painting by van Gogh appears, Ferdinand recalls the painter's madness when he decided to amputate his ear (sequence 14; *A-S*, 85; W, 52).[2] Madness ramifies into images and language and even draws strange lines of division through the film, such that the moonlight illuminating the couple in one of their sole moments of bliss (sequence 18; *A-S*, 88; W, 57–8) confers on the screen a cobalt *lunacy* that perhaps anticipates the color Ferdinand smears over his face before he dynamites his body.

Madness seems to be the reason that rules over the interstitial areas of the image and sound tracks. The word *fou* seems to follow the anagrammatical logic that Godard exploits with truculent brilliance in other films of the same period, in which intertitles display words inhabiting the mannequins of other words. Ferdinand remarks to Marianne, when they drive along the periphery of Paris, "*Dans envie il y a vie. J'avais envie, j'étais en vie*" (sequence 8; *A-S*, 76; W, 35). His penchant for anagrams makes it licit to see the beginning of the protagonist's folly when he utters, about having been fired from a position in the media business, "Well, now! I'll sue them at the TV Studio for having kicked me out" [*pour m'avoir* foutu *à la porte*] (sequence 4; *A-S*, 74; cf. W, 25), meaning that he has already gone mad because the symptom is in the word; or else, whenever he or Marianne sighs *"Je m'en* fous," it could be that madness is denied by the standardized – as if it were a product of Standard Oil – quality of the cliché denoting indifference. Madness becomes an exhilarating process of combination that even flashes between one idiom and another. In his cameo appearance at the cocktail party, Samuel Fuller growls (in English) to his interlocutors, "I'm an American film director. My name is Samuel Fuller. I'm here to make a picture in Paris, called *The Flowers of Evil."* When his interpreter explains to Ferdinand, who wonders what the man is saying, she responds, "It's Mr. Samuel Fu . . . Fuller" [*C'est Monsieur Samuel* Fu . . . *Fuller*] (sequence 6; *A-S,* 75; cf. W, 28), and her Gallic inflection of the director's American name turns him into "Samuel *fou . . . foulaire,"* a man whose name is inhabited by madness, and who, furthermore, is filming something *fou* (if we detect the phoneme and the grapheme in the gap discerned between *"fleurs"* and *"flowers"*).

In this way madness moves between images and words all through *Pierrot.* It inhabits single letters that acquire the aspect of a hieroglyphic style that striates the images and the dialogue.[3] Different reiterations of the signifier *fou* bind the story about a man's love gone crazy in a post-*noir* condition to material matters of language and visibility. The cursory presence of visual and aural shards of the title, which continually waft about the film – like flotsam – signal how *Pierrot* requires us to grasp its language as an expression that moves multilaterally. It also offers some telling clues about a broader context of language and idiocy that informs the style of *Pierrot* in general.

CRAZED LANGUAGE: THEORY

Pierrot makes its "madness" a function of these transverse connections and ruptures that belong to a hieroglyphic style. Utterances and markings exceed the control of the film and its spectator. They share much with the tenor of what Michel Foucault had been writing at a time synchronous with Godard's initial work on *Pierrot.* Two of his early essays seem to serve as a blue-

Marianne-Pierrot's sea of madness

print for the film. In "La folie, absence de l'œuvre" language goes
mad when "languages are folded upon themselves, in other
words, expressing in their statements the idiom in which they
express those statements."[4] Madness in language is "the irruptive
figure of the signifier," that is less what reveals or refers to a concealed meaning than a

> figure that retains and suspends meaning, that maps out a void in
> which a statement is nothing more than the always unfulfilled
> possibility that one given meaning might happen to come and
> inhabit it, or another, or yet another still. Maybe infinitely. Mad-
> ness opens a lacunary reserve that designates and brings to light
> this empty space where language and speech are folded together,
> each being formed by the other and stating nothing other than
> their ever-silent bond. (418)

Language goes mad when it makes clear its capacity to designate the empty form that gives birth to a writing – of literature, film, painting, music – or the place where it is continually missing, but also, from which it can never be concealed. Foucault calls the site the "double incompatibility of the work and madness, the blind spot of their possibility to each other and of their mutual exclusion" (419).

Foucault reaches these conclusions after locating a rift between social codes that delineate madness from sanity and the practice of language itself. In the practice of language interdictions in speech often get blurred or become imperceptible in the habit of everyday use. Yet the language that conveys the prevailing social codes tends to impose – modestly, almost invisibly – restrictions of the same order. Foucault delineates three axes by which practices of speech demarcate madness from meaning. The first concerns surveillance of grammatical errors or infractions of linguistic codes in pedagogical situations; then come expressions of profanation that raise the question about when, where, and how blasphemy can be uttered; the meanings that words arouse can refer to different regimes of censure. Finally – and most important for Godard – when speech of one accepted code is transposed onto another, "whose key is given in that very speech, such that the latter is replicated inside of itself, it states what it says, but it adds a *silent surplus* that ventriloquizes what it says and codes it according to the way it is said" (416). Nothing forbidden is communicated through the discourse; rather, an "essential recess" opens the language from within and up to an infinite degree. In this fourth area it matters little what is said or meant: suddenly speech witnesses "this obscure and central liberation" in its very crux, and "an uncontrollable flight to a dark point that no culture can ever immediately accept. Not in its meaning, not in its verbal matter, but in its *play* speech of this kind becomes transgressive" (ibid.).

These conclusions come on the heels of one of Foucault's precocious studies of the contemporary novel, "Le langage de l'espace."[5] A madness of language is palpable when it becomes a spatial object, a spatial thing *[chose d'espace]*. Writing of the

French *nouveau roman*,[6] he remarks that the recent novels display "with a methodical rigor the play of verbal space at odds with things" (412). Space invades these novels not from without – as what is being represented by words referring to situations or places in a common gazetteer – but from within their own form. Each page of these novels constitutes a verbal grid, a safeguard *[garde-fou]* that displays an expanse of words lurking behind, in a whisper *[murmure]* (412), indicating that the power of language derives from its being "woven" (411) with space. The juxtaposition of "Le langage de l'espace" (published in April 1964) and "La folie, l'absence de l'œuvre" (which appeared a month later) underscores how much what Foucault calls the madness of language depends on its being perceived in correlation with space. Space "opens" an otherwise closed, unquestioned, or impermeable relation of discourse to meaning. It gives rise to a liberation of meaning from the conventions of pragmatic exchange.

As is clear by the way the word *fou* moves over the surface of the film, what inspires Godard owes to unlikely correlations of space and time. Everything in the film happens at once. In the mosaic of images and discourses, any given fragment appears to be the interstice of an infinite number of others, coextensive, that are not set in any prearranged narrative compartments (even if sequences can designate developments in the story). By inventing these relations of space, discourse, and madness, the film becomes a theoretical object. It becomes what philosophers have called interpretive wrenches or screwdrivers in an analytical "toolbox" crucial for a critical analysis of culture.[7]

In this direction a closer reading of the hieroglyphic style brings into view "the lacunary reserve" of images and discourses of *Pierrot* in their broader relation with time and space. The madness of *Pierrot* assumes the form of mystical explosions of image and discourse that at once produce and eradicate space. Like the fireworks that illuminate the evening sky (sequence 7; A-S, 76; W, 34–5), each is a blitz of apprehension that becomes an *event* in which the spectator grasps insight about what language cannot say or indicate. What would have been uniquely eventful – the theme or the aim – in a classical film, such as a sublime apprehension of the world and its infinity, instead gets infinitized.

The event of *Pierrot*'s madness is concerned, notes Gilles Deleuze, with time perceived not as succession or simultaneity, but, like space itself, as an active permanence. The film replicates the sublimity of perception, affect, and sensation by establishing a hazardous interstitiality among images and sounds in place of cohering webbings of analogical form.

> This is not an operation of association, but of differentiation, as mathematicians say, of disappearance, as physicists say: given one potential, another one has to be chosen, not any whatever, but in such a way that a difference of potential is established between the two, which will be productive of a third or of something new.[8]

The interstice becomes a critical, "irreducible difference" that allows resemblances to be plotted out. In this sense the cinematic madness and the mystical undercurrent of the film constitute the interstitial relations that emerge as soon as a cognitive stress is placed on the gap between the sound and image tracks. "Interstices thus proliferate everywhere, in the visual image, in the sound image, between the sound image and the visual image."[9] The interstice is not rational (insofar as in classical cinema it would be an interruption in a routine, *a via rupta*, that affirms a seamless order by virtue of counterpoint), but *irrational*, belonging neither to what precedes or follows, or what may be spatially adjacent. Deleuze insists that the irrational quality of the line of rupture in Godard isolates "an unthought in thought . . . an irrational proper to thought, an outside point beyond the outside world, but capable of restoring our belief in the world."[10]

This interpretation taps into the lacunary reserve of language, but also into an element essential to a mystical enterprise in which reiterated reflections of an unknown quantity (what Deleuze lists as Orson Welles's *unutterable* [inévocable], Alain Robbe-Grillet's *inexplicable*, Alain Resnais's *undecidable*, Marguerite Duras's *impossible*, and Godard's *incommensurable*) depend on the presence of an "all," a *tout*, of an "incompossible" world that somehow is discerned only in and about the interstitial relation of elements infinitely juxtaposed to one another. The mad "vision," then, of *Pierrot* depends on a proliferation of ruptures about and through quasi-indiscernible figures that are reflective of an improbable and even impossible totality whose perimeters cannot be grasped, and that cannot be imagined in any proportional terms such as those that would tie a microcosm (Pierrot, who indeed describes himself as a question mark on the horizon of the world) to a macrocosm (the earth and the heavens).

CRAZED LANGUAGE: PRACTICE

To see how the "world" is glimpsed in its impossibility, or how it becomes a function of interstitial relations of language and image, we can now turn to the beginning of the film.[11] The title and the first four shots play out the relation. After two titles bear, respectively, *Visa de contrôle cinématographique n° 29 397* and *René Pigères et Gérard Beytout présentent,* the credits are born from spatial sites defined by the alphabet and a colored scheme of letters. When finally constituted, the title reads:

JEAN-PAUL BELMONDO

ET

ANNA KARINA

DANS

PIERROT LE FOU

UN FILM DE

JEAN-LUC GODARD

The words literally "take place" as the appearance of the letter A four times in red (in the first, third, fourth, and seventh line), is followed, at short intervals, by the others, in accord with an alphabetical order (B of BELMONDO; C of LUC; D of DANS; E of JEAN, ET, PIERROT, DE, and JEAN; etc.). The title appears to be connected with the director when the two R's of PIERROT appear synchronously with the R of GODARD below.

A cohering scatter of characters: the seven tiers of letters emerge from a state of nascence, but as they dot the screen, they also suggest that they are liable to be recombined according to different algorithms. Given or virtual words of the title can meld into others. The pattern indicates that a madness inhabiting its process will be related to the subsequent intertitles and hieroglyphic pieces, such as the brand names of gasoline (TOTAL, ESSO) or cars (a Ford "Galaxy") that will shift and shuffle letters and their referents.[12]

Soon after the credits the voice *off* declares, "*space* reigns" (sequence 1; *A-S*, 72; W, 24), and that the latter will appose film's language to a boundless extension ("the world") that pervades the image but remains inaccessible to the figures who move through it.[13] The first shot records a tennis game in a sun-splashed park that is called in question by the uttering of *crépuscule* in the words *off* that read: *Velázquez, après cinquante ans, ne peignait plus jamais une chose définie. Il errait autour des objets avec l'air et le crépuscule* ["After he had reached the age of fifty, Velázquez no longer painted anything concrete and precise"]. The second shot, a countershot of the entirety of the tennis court, is accompanied by words that continue to contravene the diurnal picture of the women at play: . . . *il surprenait dans l'ombre et la transparence des fonds les palpitations colorées dont il faisait le centre invisible de sa symphonie silencieuse. Il ne saisissait plus dans le monde que* . . . ["In the shimmering of shadows he caught unawares the colored palpitations which he transformed into the visible heart of his symphony of silence. He no longer grasped in the world . . ."]. The word *monde* is heard just as the third shot displays, in silence, at the outset of the second sequence, the outside of a bookstore named (by an implicit intertitle in the image) "Le Meilleur des Mondes." Beneath it we see Jean-Paul Belmondo purchasing a book in front of the store. The "colored palpitations" can refer (as they also may not) to the red and blue letters that had spelled out the name of the film and its leading actor. "Belmondo" in the credits becomes suffused in the dark "world" evoked in the quotation, but such that the words from art history both bind and keep detached the relation between the tennis ball as miniature globe, Velázquez's *world* of "mysterious exchanges," the image and voice

of "Bel*mondo*," the allusion to Leibniz's (and *Candide*'s) best of all
possible "worlds" in the name of the bookstore, and the universe
of graphemes that make up the letters of the credits.

At this moment the spectator who has "read" and seen the
birth of the language of the title of the film intuits that the text is
taken from Élie Faure's well-known *Histoire de l'art*.[14] But inasmuch
as the author, to this point unnamed, remains a mystery, the
advent of the memory of "Élie Faure" is inflected – in the dialogi-
cal area of language being described in the quoted text – by a
homonym. *Et lis [lit] fort* ["please read alertly"] advises the spectator to decipher the given images by seeing how language inheres
in them but skitters and scatters over their surface. Thus we are
enjoined to perceive their "world" intensely. In the fourth shot, a
long shot of a port is seen at a crepuscular moment, at dawn or in
the late evening. The image responds to what was announced in
the quotation accompanying the first shot in daylight. Suddenly a
connection is made when Faure's description of Velázquez (*off*, so
far without any grounding in the frame) seems to confirm the
murky image that follows: . . . *les échanges mystérieux qui font
pénétrer les uns dans les autres les formes et les tons, par un progrès
secret et continu dont aucun heurt, aucun sursaut ne dénonce ou n'inter-
rompt la démarche. L'espace règne* ["those mysterious exchanges
whose forms and tones interpenetrate, through a secret and continuous advance unimpeded or uninterrupted by any clash or
shock. Space reigns . . ."].

What Belmondo might have been "thinking" in these words
while buying books at the *Le Meilleur des Mondes* virtually bleeds
into the sunset, but also into the words (and initial bars of omi-
nous music):

> *C'est comme une onde aérienne qui glisse sur les surfaces, s'imprègne de
> leurs émanations invisibles pour les définir et les modeler, et emporter
> partout ailleurs comme un parfum, comme un écho d'elles qu'elle dis-
> perse sur toute l'étendue environnante en poussière impondérable* ["It's
> as if an aerial wave were gliding over the surfaces, impregnated
> with their visible emanations, modeling them and endowing
> them with form, then carrying them off everywhere else like a

perfume, like an echo, which would thus be dispersed over all the surrounding expanse like an imponderable dust"].

In the syncopations of the images and discourse the final words – *poussière impondérable* – refer back both to a regime of infinitely scattering worlds (in which dust is a privileged figure of multiplication), and quite possibly, also to Faure's own descriptions of the infinitizing qualities of time in cinema. In the precocious essays on "Cineplastics," he appeals to dust and pulverized stone to describe the awe a viewer experiences over transformations of time and matter through montage.[15] The multiplied figures of the world *[monde]* become molecularized in the echo and the literal wave of the *onde aérienne* that pervades the world of Velázquez heard *off*.

The fifth shot extends the relation of the title to the "world" being brought into view, summarized, multiplied, and dispersed through other shards of language that atomized in the image-field. Interior, at night, but in the glare of bright light, a close-up shows Belmondo in a bathtub, smoking a cigarette (an ashtray and an opened pack of cigarettes are on the edge of the tub just behind him) and continuing to read aloud the words from the *Histoire de l'art: Le monde où il vivait était triste* ["The world he lived in was sad"]. Confused with Velázquez, Belmondo bathes in a bookish world conveyed through quotation on the sound track. On the image track, the pictures of art works of the West on the front and back cover of the paperback become "windows" of monadlike totalities related to the particles of dust, ash, and smoke on the edge of, or wafting above the tub. Each picture is suspended in a molecular realm implied by the water, atmosphere, and the quotation concerning the *onde aérienne* and *émanations visibles*.[16] Yet try as we may to find a connection between one world and the other, no motivating relation comes forward: as cinematic hermeneuts we see ourselves going mad in our desire to make connections stronger than those of interstices and haphazard contiguities.

An immediate instant of silence is marked on the sound track by the rustle of a page being turned as Belmondo looks toward the screen and remarks in the first deictic expression of the film: *Écoute ça, petite fille* ["Listen to that, my little girl!"]. What Belmondo begs the girl (not yet seen, but soon entering the frame as the camera pulls back) to *hear* is what we *see* in a memory-image of Velázquez, of *Las Meninas,* the painting that in our century – and especially in the writings of Michel Foucault at the time of the filming of *Pierrot le fou*[17] – captures many of the paradoxes of reason, madness, and the optical traits of language. The *petite fille* translates into human form an allusion to *Las Meninas.* A childish sensibility is brought forward to underscore the "lacunary reserve" of possible connections. They are further emphasized by the paradoxical moment of contact and rupture when the little girl's bare hands extend to the tub, in proximity to Pierrot's bare shoulder, as the sound track intones: *Un esprit nostalgique flotte, mais on ne voit ni la laideur, ni la tristesse, ni le sens funèbre et cruel de cette enfance écrasée* ["A spirit of nostalgia prevailed. But we see none of the ugliness or sadness or any of the signs of gloom and cruelty of this crippled infancy"]. As the shot continues, a voice with Italian inflection – that we discover belongs to Pierrot's wife – exclaims, "You're mad *[fou]* to read to her things like that!" The voice thus reiterates a fragment of the title of the film, but in such a way that the visible and mute sign in the credits is iterated in the speech. Her remark makes apparent the fortuitous relation that holds between the title and the sign of the world. It also shows how the discourse of *Pierrot* is inflected with a baroque tradition of painting.

For the shots that follow the title, a schema might help to sum up the way the world *[monde],* literalized, moves through the languages of the film:

SHOTS	TITLE	1–2	3	4	5
IMAGE		tennis ball/ women	[Bel*mondo*]	crepuscular world	picture window/ tub/ashtray
GRAPHS	Bel*mondo*		*Meilleur des* Mondes		Élie Faure, *Histoire de l'art*
VOICE			*monde*	*poussière impondérable onde aérienne*	*le monde où il vivait*

In the space between the incipit of the title, when *fou* is first seen in silence, and the first instance (voice *off*) of the utterance of *fou* heard, the greater "worlds" of the film have been established. The scope of the narrative that follows moves through the linguistic and painterly references concealed – but obviously visible – in the world of sexual isolation delineated between the first two shots. Shots 1 and 2 seem to replicate the Hollywood system of shot/ countershot. The two views are on a tennis court. We witness a *playground* in which women bounce an icon of the world across a gridded net. Shots 3 and 4 isolate the male in an ethereal fantasy of words, letters, forms, and tones. Viewers familiar with the relation of the New Wave to the history of film and history in general recall that the tennis court is a *locus classicus* of the birth of desire and vision.[18] A scene we can call "primal" – at once for the birth of desire and the drive to produce montage – is brought forward in the memories it elicits and in the same isolation and relation of sexual power contained within the reference to *Les Mistons* and signs of war that interfere with *Las Meninas*.

The writing of the credits, however, calls into question the privilege of a merely cinematic allusion to an earlier stage in the evolution of New Wave cinema. When the letters of the title appear in alphabetical progression, **a**, **b**, **c**, and **d** appear in red before the **e** of "Pierrot" is seen in blue. The name of the film is spelled out in blue, whereas the other verbal material is in red. In the English version a white subtitle ("Pierrot Gone Mad"), set along the lower horizontal edge of the frame, establishes a tricolor motif on the black background.[19] The French screenplay notes that as soon as the words of the title are established, "Only *Pierrot le fou* is written in blue. The rest of the title disappears, then *le*, then all the letters, except the two *O*'s that in turn are extinguished one after the other" (*A-S*, 72). The initial, divided, angular, traditionally "compassed" letter, the A conveys things red.[20]

The spectator who has a working knowledge of French literature is baited to murmur, in response to what he or she perceives of the first letter, "*A rouge.*" Is it *ar(t) rouge* (red art) or *art ou/où je* ("art or me" or "art where I")? Is it merely "a red" (in the bilingual sense of something red, such as an A)? No sooner than the virtual meanings are declined does the most fragrantly colored of all French poems come forward in travesty. Rimbaud's celebrated "Voyelles" begins not with a red A but with combinations of colors and letters (which are seen later in the film), that are somewhat other:

> *A noir, E blanc, I rouge, U vert, O bleu: voyelles,*
> *Je dirai quelque jour vos naissances latentes:*
> *A, noir corset velu des mouches éclatantes. . . .*[21]

Here the "reserve" described in Foucault's "La folie, absence de l'œuvre," remains for both Godard and Rimbaud a maddeningly vibrant sensation of language in its purest movement (that is, emotion). At its very beginning, then, the color field of the text of the title alludes to the famous poem that the cinematic medium is rewriting. *A, rouge* is a miniature hieroglyph that will drive the composition in the direction of the tension between a political and historical color field (red/white/blue) and a purely tonal relation that begins with colors which precede and exceed meaning. The quasi-retinal suspension of Rimbaud's world of colored letters returns when all the graphemes disappear except, in the last instant, the two blue O's of *Pierrot le fou.*[22] The riddle that seems to be tendered in the visual overlay of letters, images, and texts in the first five shots is reiterated by means of corresponding tones that are literally bled into other sequences. This initial swarm of fragmentary signs that cohere and disperse, that capture and disseminate the "world" of the film, recurs with uncanny consistency.

INTERPRETATION GOING CRAZY

To see how the color red suffuses the film we need only recall sequence 37. Despondent, Ferdinand is seated on a railroad track that extends horizontally across the frame, in front of a river and a scrubby pine grove. He mutters in the long shot, as a train is heard approaching, "Ah! what a dreadful five in the afternoon! . . .

Blood, I do not want to see blood . . . Ah! what a dreadful five in
the afternoon . . . I do not want to see it . . . I do not want to see
the blood . . . Ah! what a dreadful five in the afternoon" (*A-S*, 97;
W, 81). He is quoting Garcia Lorca's "Lament for Ignacio Sánchez
Mejías," a poem written during the bloodshed of the Spanish Civil
War. The words are remembered when sequence 38 begins with a
countertilt of the port of Toulon (indicated by the ships of the
French fleet at anchor in the background) that catches a mast of a
boat flying two French flags. A downward pan catches two mili-
tary vessels in the harbor, then fixes on flotsam and detritus float-
ing by the quay from which, in the next shot, Ferdinand is seen
seated, his back to a wall, reading the newspaper *France-Soir*. The
third-person narration that tells of the hero's travels is uttered in
clauses that alternate the voices of Marianne and Ferdinand, as if
the two lovers were *off*, together and apart, in another space, peer-
ing upon the images constructed by the vocal rhythm that inflects
the image. The relation of the voices to the image emphasizes the
nature of the world and affect being shown:

IMAGE TRACK	SOUND TRACK
sky, mast, boat, flags (extreme long shot) pan to naval vessels	Marianne: *On retrouve Ferdinand qui débarque à la gare de . . .* Ferdinand: *Toulon.* Marianne: *On le voit qui flâne dans les rues et sur le port. Il habite . . .*
pan to flotsam and detritus (medium shot)	Ferdinand: *Au 'Little Palace Hotel'.*
pan to Pierrot reading *France-Soir* (medium shot)	Marianne: *Il cherche . . .* Ferdinand: *Marianne.* Marianne: *Et ne la trouve pas. Les jours passent. L'après-midi, Ferdinand dort quelquefois dans les cinémas permanents. Il continue à écrire son journal. . . .*[23]

An insert shows Pierrot in profile, in a medium shot, lighting a
cigarette in front of a poster on which are written in bold white
letters on a red background, s.o.s. A second insert displays a draw-
ing of the face of young Rimbaud about which are pasted the let-

ters O (blue), U (tan), and, below the poet's mouth, I (red). The image and the dialogue are aligned thus:

IMAGE TRACK	SOUND TRACK
Ferdinand in front of poster and s.o.s. (medium shot)	Ferdinand: *Car les mots au milieu des ténèbres ont un étrange pouvoir d'éclairement . . .* Marianne: *De la chose qu'ils nomment. En effet . . .*
portrait of Rimbaud with colored letters on his face (close-up)	Ferdinand: *Même si elle est compromise dans l'horizon quotidien. . . .* Marianne: *Le langage souvent ne retient que la pureté.*[24]

When *éclairement* ["enlightenment"] is uttered, the "illumination" of Rimbaud is seen in the portrait and its collage of colored vowels. There follows an insert of a pen, writing in red ink, in what would be Ferdinand's journal:

> Marianne
>   Ariane   mer   [Ariadne   sea]
> âme   amer   [soul   bitter]
>   arme   [arm]

The entry becomes spatialized by the calligrammatic placement of the fragments of Marianne's name that are fixed once the pen stops moving. No hand is present that would identify who is writing, nor is it quite clear if the words are being written in the dark of a movie theater, as implied in the report conveyed by Marianne's voice.

Because of the process set in motion since the credits and the first four shots, an amazing itinerary of language and images has taken place from the end of sequence 37 through sequence 38. The allusion to Lorca's haunting poem becomes Godard's signature through the allusive presence of Charles Baudelaire's "Harmonie du soir," a tonal poem of sixteen lines that associates the red sunset with the clotting of blood.[25] Who or what is producing the poem cannot be ascertained. It resembles one of Guillaume Apollinaire's cubist *calligrammes,* the source of inspiration having already been noted in sequence 19, when Ferdinand invokes (*off*), as he walks along the beach with Marianne, "A poet, called revolver . . ." to which Marianne responds (*off*), "Robert Browning" (*A-S,* 88; W, 58), alluding both to the English romantic poet and to Apollinaire's calligram, "Éventail des saveurs," which includes a verbal icon of a Browning automatic pistol.[26] Here, however, language being spatialized produces movement and its color, the virtue Fuller had identified in a good film: "In one word . . . emotion" (sequence 6; *A-S,* 75; W, 33), or that Godard is conveying with explosiveness, flamboyance, and force. E*motion* – that is, movement – follows the broken lines we draw between the audible and visible formations of languages and images.

The memory of Baudelaire's vermilion crepuscule, politicized and renewed by way of Lorca, stages the intensification of verbal sensation with the insert of the red s.o.s. poster and the "red I" of Rimbaud's portrait. What might have referred to a Morse code of pure dots and dashes, that ventriloquizes Ferdinand's plight as he smokes a cigarette, unaware of the image that is speaking (for) him, also becomes, in the Spanish world of Velázquez or of pure metaphysics, an affirmation of whatever is . . . is, *Eso es,* that refers back to the mire of international capitalism (Standard Oil or esso) and its multinational power (Total) that the hero sought to evade by burrowing into writing and sleeping in movie theaters.[27]

When Rimbaud's portrait appears, it becomes the mute speaker of the dialogue between Marianne and Ferdinand about the "enlightening" powers of words seen or heard in darkness. The colored letters co-respond – again in the sense of Baudelaire's sonnet, "Correspondances," a cornerstone of *Les Fleurs du mal* that inspired Rimbaud's "Voyelles" – to the savor of language *before* its meaning fixes the word into place. The colors of the letters constitute a reserve, a fortuitous madness preexisting the rigor mortis of a "work" or an *œuvre.* The primary colors of the letters adorning Rimbaud's portrait turn the writing into a field of tones and erotic sensations exceeding a correlation of words to things. The cinematic apparatus is renewing but extending in new directions and countless ways what "Voyelles" had initiated. Ferdinand's simple poem that declines the virtues and vices of Marianne shows how the style of *Pierrot* makes language regress to its most crystalline and timelessly mythic expression. When the image track shows that "Ariane" emerges from Marianne, the graphemes disperse in various directions, but at the same time, a classical, "Mediterranean" space of tragedy is localized in both the coming of the "sea" *[mer]* that the penned letters in red are anticipating, and in the reference to an almost incestuous eros that the film invests in itself, by way of *Ariane,* a name that can either be associated with the model of a car (such as a Citroën DS or a *Déesse*), Velázquez's painting of tapestry weavers, or, in Racine's *Phèdre,* the tragic protagonist's projection of her own longings onto her sister, represented in one of the purest moments of French poetry:

Ariane, ma sœur, de quelle amour blessée
Vous mourûtes au bord où vous fûtes laissée?[28]

Marianne, the personification of Republican France, functions as an anagram that simultaneously invokes the names of baroque figures and classical deities. Her name refers to the rhetoric of seduction that Ronsard practiced by reading *aimer* in *Marie* in the *Continuation des amours* of 1556 as well as to the Ariadne written on the screen.[29] In the "anna-gram" Marianne produces *Aimer* [to love] and *rimer* [to rhyme] *Anna.* As the language of the film goes mad by increasing its referential field, its webbing becomes progressively constrictive. The pen that writes independently of any character discovers, scripting a fragmentation, the very elements of the narrative: Marianne indeed weaves Ferdinand in a "spider's stratagem," she figures in the seascape of a Mediterranean archipelago, she brings bitterness to the souls of those in her midst, and she is *armed.* The scansion of the name follows the Rimbaldian principles that inaugurated the credits, the final three words being cued in accord with the red A that was first seen in the image field of the title.

When Marianne indeed does become an avatar of "Ariadne" sealing the fate of Ferdinand, a "spider's strategy" is made manifest. In sequence 44 (*A-S*, 103; W, 96), an enormous net falls on a car driven by a group of gangsters. As the men wrest themselves free of the mesh, Marianne, armed with a rifle equipped with a telescopic sight, *spies* on the scene from behind a tree trunk, takes aim, and catches her victims in the crosshairs. Three sequences later, in her next encounter with Ferdinand, Marianne is seen in a bowling alley, lifting a ball above her chest. The images extend the signs that had inaugurated the film and inflected the opening shots. The ambush by means of a telescopic rifle can refer to the ending of *High Sierra* (Raoul Walsh, 1941) that inspired *A bout de souffle/Breathless* (1960) in which, in a variation on the fate of Orpheus and Eurydice, the protagonist is double-crossed into being shot by a high-powered rifle equipped with a telescope. In *Pierrot* the iris shot that displays Marianne's victim in the three crosshairs takes the shape of a medieval "T-and-O" map, a schematic *mappamundi* of the three known continents of the world. In the graphic configuration of the shot a miniature totality resides in the archaic cinematic device being used to establish Marianne's deadly "point of view." The sudden irruption of a figure of the "world" in the frame would be a cartographical fantasy if, in the moments that follow, Marianne were not seen in an emblem in which she holds a bowling ball as if it were a "world in her hands." In the dialogue Ferdinand asks Marianne to kiss him, to which she replies, *Pas devant tout le monde* ["Not in front of the whole world"] (sequence 47; *A-S*, 104; cf. W, 98).

The inserts that record the writing of Ferdinand's journal, or the cutaways to posters or portraits, like that of Rimbaud adorned with colored vowels, renew the tradition of the intertitle, a variant of the hieroglyph. A tradition is renewed and rewritten, but now so that the "world" of the film continues to exceed itself within the relation of images, colors, letters, and inherited symbols. A paratactic order of world figures indicates the dispersive nature of Godard's language. If Jacques Derrida's theories of language can be grafted onto the effects of scattering being followed here, a force

Marianne-Ariadne's spider's net

of *dissemination* is marked in the relation between the icons of world figures that expand the space of the film and the shards of discourse which include spoken language, written signs, and objects.[30]

Language goes mad anywhere and everywhere. In sequence 17 (*A-S*, 86; W, 56) – possibly the most memorable for a majority of viewers – Pierrot drives a stolen American convertible into the sea. In the "mad" language of the film, a tension is established between the name and image of the car, a "Ford Galaxy," and the cosmic icons that accompany it. The car had been erected, as if it were a sculpture, on the garage lift, in full aesthetic display. Suddenly, however, the "galaxy" becomes the space that Ferdinand wishes to reach by way of love and a discovery of literature; its solar system is already evident in the constellations of hubcaps, tires, headlamps, and circular taillights. When a panoramic shot follows the Ford driving off the road and splashing into the sea, the great spray of water molecularizes the "Galaxy," offering to the imagination an explosive froth of globules anticipating the scatter of the hero's own body when he blows himself into the atmosphere at the end of the film.

In sequence 44 Ferdinand laments that too much is happening at once *[Y a trop d'événements à la fois]* (*A-S*, 101; W, 94). If *Pierrot* is an event that questions the way we read images and languages in the history and practice of cinema, it may be because the film produces an excess – or a reserve – of events everywhere in its form. If that is the case, then Pierrot, a pilgrim and a traveler, becomes the cipher for what begins in the credits of the film. In "Let's Talk About *Pierrot*," Godard quips that "making *Pierrot le fou* consisted of living through an event. An event is made up of other events which one happens to come across. In general . . . making a film is a comparable adventure" (N&M, 224, translation modified; B, 269). By way of conclusion we can say that the adventure of *Pierrot* begins with the serial inscription of the red A. There begins the process of a continuous rift of discourse and image. In the rift a constant atomization or dissemination of shapes – like the spray of water when the "Galaxy" goes into the sea, or the blast of fire and smoke when Pierrot blows himself to smithereens – takes place, in a creation of a hieroglyph and new cinematic spaces.

NOTES

1. By "sequence" is meant each setting whose time (day or night) and place (inside or outside) is marked in bold typeface in the French edition of the scenario. The screenplay in *L'Avant-Scène* includes fifty-two sequences.

2. On the sound track the frequent recurrence of the identity of *fou* and *fous* hides a discrepancy in meaning. *Foutre* (whence the slang expression *je m'en fous*), a popular and figurative variant of *ficher* (reaching back to *figere*, to "attach" or "fix in place") has no etymological connection with *fou* (from the Latin *follis*, a bag or balloon filled with air), but a connection is made on the signifying surface of the film when we hear the identity.

3. Gilles Deleuze, an ardent admirer of Godard, remarked that in *In Search of Lost Time* Marcel Proust replaces the world of knowledge, reason, or of "analytic expression, phonetic writing, and rational thought" with that of "hieroglyphs and ideograms" that are amphibious and multivalent (*Proust and Signs*, trans. Richard Howard [New York: George Braziller, 1972], 96). Godard's relation to the language of cinema can be likened to the way Proust rewrites the language of the classical French novel.

4. In Michel Foucault, *Dits et écrits 1: 1954–1969*, eds. Daniel Defert and François Ewald (Paris: Gallimard, 1994), 417. Subsequent references appear in the text. All translations mine.

5. In Michel Foucault, *Dits et écrits 1: 1954–1969*. Subsequent references appear in the text. All translations mine.

6. The New Novel, championed by such writers as Alain Robbe-Grillet, came to prominence in French literature in the 1950s. See also Jill Forbes's discussion in this volume.

7. Luce Giard, "Demain déjà se donne à naître." Introduction to Michel de Certeau's essays on May 1968 in France and after, *La prise de parole et autres écrits politiques* (Paris: Seuil, 1994), 25.

8. Gilles Deleuze, *Cinema 2. The Time-Image*, trans. Hugh Tomlinson and Robert Galeta (Minneapolis: University of Minnesota Press, 1989), 179–80.

9. Ibid., 181.

10. Ibid., translation modified.

11. Invariably Deleuze's observations about Godard are unparalleled in their insight, but they tend to be as isolated or lacunary as what they describe. Close, sequential analysis is needed to test what is said about the interstice.

12. Intertitles of moving letters constitute a motif in the film, ending with a shot of Ferdinand's journal, on which, between the letters *LA* and *RT* on blue are inscribed in hand, *mo* in lowercase (sequence 52; *A-S*, 108; W, 104).

13. Pierrot states the conundrum better than might any interpretation. As he and Marianne leave the port of Toulon in a motorized yacht that churns off toward the horizon, in an extreme long shot, the hero exclaims, as if he were addressing the spectator, "I am only a huge question mark poised over the Mediterranean horizon!" *[Je suis un vaste point d'interrogation face à l'horizon mediterranéen]* (sequence 41; *A-S*, 100; W, 92).

14. The English already given here, and continued in what follows, taken from W, 23–4 and often modified, differs considerably from that of the subtitles. See also Élie Faure, *The History of Art*, Vol. 2, trans. Walter Pach (New York: Dover, 1948), 124–8 (Cf. Élie Faure, *Histoire de l'art*, Vol. 4, L'Art moderne [Paris: G. Crès et Cie, 1920], 115–20).

15. An English translation of Faure's work on cinéplastics (in which dust plays a crucial role in the associative process that the surgeon-

writer performs), is found in James Talbot (ed.), *Film Theory: An Anthology* (New York, 1970). The cinematic and molecular properties of dust are taken up extensively in Gilles Deleuze, *The Fold: Leibniz and the Baroque,* trans. Tom Conley (Minneapolis: University of Minnesota Press, 1993), Chapter 7, in which Leibniz and the event of a swarm of sensations and perceptions are melded in a quotation from Thomas de Quincey's *The Revolt of the Tartars:*

> Through the next hour, during which the gentle morning breeze had a little freshened, the dusty vapour had developed itself far and wide into the appearance of huge aerial draperies, hanging in mighty volumes from the sky to the earth. . . . But sometimes, as the wind slackened or died away, all those openings, of whatever form, in the cloudy pall would slowly close, and for a time the whole pageant was shut up from view; although the growing din, the clamours, shrieks, and groans, ascending from infuriated myriads, reported, in a language not to be misunderstood, what was going on behind the cloudy screen." (*The Fold,* 94)

16. It happens that Faure's description of Velázquez's baroque world also encapsulates much of what follows in the film: *Un roi dégénéré, des enfants malades, des idiots, des nains, des infirmes, quelques pitres monstrueux vêtus en princes qui avaient pour fonction de rire d'eux-mêmes et d'en faire rire des êtres hors la loi vivante, étreints par l'étiquette, le complot, le mensonge, liés par la confession et le remords. Aux portes, l'Autodafé, le silence* ["A degenerate king, inbred infantas, idiots, dwarfs, cripples, a few deformed clowns (as for example, *pierrots*) clothed as princes whose only job was to laugh at themselves and to amuse those lifeless outlaws who were constrained by etiquette, conspiracy, lies, and linked by confession and remorse. At the portals, the Auto-da-fé, silence . . ."]. The affinities that Godard shares with Faure merit more extensive analysis. Godard's quotation comes from the middle of Chapter 3 of Volume 4 of *Histoire de l'art,* in the pages on the Spanish Baroque. Faure dedicated the volume thus: *A Renoir* [To Renoir].

17. See Chapter 6, n. 35.

18. Truffaut's study of the birth of the male pubescent eros, *Les Mistons/The Mischief Makers* (1957), comes immediately to mind. A group of boys gaze on Bernadette Lafont's lithe and svelte body dancing on the turf of a tennis court nestled in the hills of the Vaucluse. The tennis court could also be related to another webbing of signifiers: first, as a site of combat, it can refer to what Sam Fuller, à propos of cinema in general, later calls a "battleground," and second, it can evoke the site of revolution insofar as the French viewer associates a *jeu de paume* with the Tennis Court Oaths that were crucial to the Revolution of 1789.

19. The emblematic colors of the French flag are established. In the mix of language and painting the relation arches back to Monet's famous painting (often adorning the dust jackets of textbooks of

impressionism or art history in general) of a parade on the 14th of July, in which, inverse to the credits of *Pierrot le fou,* black characters spelling out *Vive la France* emerge. Godard makes a color field emerge from the letters; Monet allows the dissonant tone of black to heighten the sensation of the mix of red, white, and blue. Both Godard and Monet allow a foreign form to intercede in their images and to bring force to them by its alterity. See also Jean-Louis Leutrat's discussion in this volume.

20. The A has traditionally been the "aleph," the letter of force (the bull), but in Godard's world it has geometrical trappings that recall the origin of visibility as *angularity,* as *Angst,* and as *anguish,* such as that with which Georges Bataille inflects the character by means of the toponym of the *Rue Angoisse* at the beginning of *Madame Edwarda.* This is carefully analyzed by Lucette Finas in *La crue: une lecture de Georges Bataille, **Madame Edwarda*** (Paris: Gallimard, 1971), 20. The hieroglyph of the A as compass that generates the construction of all subsequent representations of the world, geometrical and linguistic alike, is the subject of the neo-Platonic gloss of Geoffroy Tory in his *Champ fleury* (Paris, 1529); the political trappings of the A-as-geometer's compass is studied in Anne-Marie Lecoq, *François Ier imaginaire* (Paris: Éditions Macula, 1987).

21. Arthur Rimbaud, *Oeuvres,* eds. Suzanne Bernard and André Guyaux (Paris: Garnier, 1981), 110 [A black, E white, I red, U green, O blue: vowels//One day I will tell you your latent birth//A, black hairy corset of shining flies . . .] ("Vowels" in *Rimbaud, Complete Works, Selected Letters,* trans. Wallace Fowlie [Chicago: University of Chicago Press, 1966], 121).

22. Here the film regains its affiliation with the sonnet by indicating the presence of *O bleu,* the colored letter that becomes the "world" in all of its erotic force and infinitive virtue in the final line – that seems to sum up the attraction that Marianne Renoir's eyes hold for the lovestruck Pierrot, an avatar of the many tragic protagonists in the tradition of film noir. "Voyelles" ends as follows:

O, suprême Clairon plein des strideurs étranges,
Silences traversés des Mondes et des Anges:
– O l'Oméga, rayon violet de Ses Yeux!

[O, supreme Clarion full of strange stridor
Silences crossed by worlds and angels:
– O the Omega, violet beam from His eyes!]

The effect is all the more maddening in the translinguistic dimension of the graphic play. As the characters disappear, their dialogic virtue is underscored, at least when the *emotive* qualities of the film (which Sam Fuller extols about the medium in the cocktail party at the Espressos) are seen in reverse, in what is already *felt* in *Pierrot* le *fou.*

23. "Marianne: We meet Ferdinand again as he reaches the station at
. . . Ferdinand: Toulon. M: We see him wandering around the
streets and the harbour. He stays in . . . F: The Little Palace Hotel.
M: He is looking for . . . F: Marianne. M: He doesn't find her. Days
pass by. In the afternoons Ferdinand sometimes sleeps in the cinema. He continues to write his diary." (W, 82)

24. "F: For words in the midst of the shadows have a strange power of
enlightenment. M: Of the things they signify, in fact. F: Even if
they are compromised in day-to-day life. M: Language often retains
only purity" (ibid., translation modified).

25. Charles Baudelaire, *Les Fleurs du mal*, ed. Antoine Adam (Paris: Gar-
nier, 1961), 52 (XLVII in the sequence that Baudelaire established)
(cf. "The Harmony of Evening" in *The Flowers of Evil*, trans. James
McGowan [Oxford: Oxford University Press, 1993], 97). Lorca and
Baudelaire vary in terms of Faure's evocation of Velázquez. Thierry
Jousse notes that Deleuze's sense of affective molecularization is
captured in Godard's quotation of Lorca's line, in "D comme
Deleuze," *Cahiers du cinéma* 495 (1995): 26.

26. Thus:

> *Attols singuliers*
> *de brownings quel*
> > *goût*
> > *de viv*
> > *re Ah!*

In Guillaume Apollinaire, *Oeuvres poétiques*, eds. Marcel Adéma and
Michel Décaudin (Paris: Gallimard/Pléiade, 1965), 298. Cf. "Fan of
Flowers," in *Calligrammes*, trans. Anne Hyde Greet (Berkeley: Uni-
versity of California Press, 1980), 309:

> Fantastic atolls
> of revolvers what
> > a taste
> > for liv
> > ing Ah!

27. In a probing study of the politics of the anagrammar of *Pierrot*,
Thomas Odde notes an obsession with the letters O and S that associate ESSO with a kind of "petrolglyph" in which are written O.S.S.,
"Oasis," and S.O.S. The displays of letters "do not introduce utter
chaos into signification. Rather, they ask the viewer to find the
structure in chaos *by reading the film differently*." "Godard's Petro-
glyphic Cinema: *Pierrot le fou* and Economies of Writing," unpublished M.A. thesis, University of Florida (1996), 82 (emphasis his).

28. *Phèdre* (I, iii), in Racine, *Théâtre complet*, ed. Maurice Rat (Paris: Garnier, 1960), 551. Cf. *Phaedra* in Jean Racine, *Four Greek Plays*, trans.
R. C. Knight (Cambridge: Cambridge University Press), 117: "Love
left thee dying, sweet sister Ariadne, Lying forsaken by the alien
waters."

29. Henri and Catherine Weber (eds.), *Les "Amours" de Ronsard* (Paris: Garnier Frères, 1963), 175: *Marie, qui voudroit vostre beau nom tourner//Il trouveroit Aimer: aimez-moi donq, Marie* ["Marie, whoever seeks to turn your beautiful name//Would find Aimer: therefore love me, Marie"].

30. In his *Dissemination,* trans. Barbara Johnson (Chicago: University of Chicago Press, 1982), à propos of Théophile Gautier's *Pierrot posthume,* Jacques Derrida shows that the writer as mime – and, it could be added, the filmmaker – "represents nothing, imitates nothing, does not have to conform to any prior referent with the aim of achieving adequation or verisimilitude" (205), a point that leads to the concept of dissemination, replacing a hermeneutics of polysemy (262).

5 *Pierrot le fou* and Post–New Wave French Cinema

Pierrot le fou marks a turning point in Godard's career and a challenge to the New Wave aesthetic. Although clearly a film of the 1960s, it is also the link between his major early films, *A bout de souffle/Breathless* (1959) and *Le Mépris/Contempt* (1963), and the seminal post-1968 works *Tout va bien* (1972), *Sauve qui peut (la vie)/Every Man for Himself* (1979), and *Passion* (1982). In its exploration of shifting attitudes toward the United States, it documents the decade of rapid change that rendered the France of 1964 unrecognizable to that of 1974, and in its investigation of conceptions of authorship, narrative, and genre predicts the ruins of one aesthetic and the birth of another, signaling the visual and thematic changes that distinguish the "après *nouvelle vague*" from the *nouvelle vague*.[1]

THE AMERICAN CHALLENGE

The cinema embodied all the ambiguities of French attitudes toward the United States in the postwar period, portraying the U.S. both as a vibrant source of social, economic, and cultural modernity, and as a ruthless colonial power bent on destroying France's cultural specificity. This accounts for the wry confrontation between old-fashioned French gangsters and new-fangled Americanized villains in French films of the 1950s, which often depicted, in thinly disguised fictional form, a fact of French life in the aftermath of the war, acutely experienced by Godard's generation as a colonial occupation.[2] By tracing the evolution of French attitudes toward America and the way these were inscribed in cinema, we can begin to understand some of the more elliptical moments of *Pierrot le fou* and what they signify in the context of Godard's oeuvre.

As a critic for *Cahiers du cinéma*, Godard had always attributed a world cultural role to Hollywood, claiming, somewhat provocatively, that its "classicism" was analogous to the "universalism" of French literature in the eighteenth century.[3] As a filmmaker he paid tribute to the seductive influence of Hollywood by reworking, in an obviously minor key, American genres such as the thriller and the musical and creating characters who imagine themselves to be actors in American films. The "anxiety of influence," as Harold Bloom called it,[4] was given full expression in New Wave films that saw Hollywood both as an agent for the destruction of the European tradition of high art (*Le Mépris, Tirez sur le pianiste/Shoot the Piano Player* [François Truffaut, 1960]) and as a model and a source. This explains why both Godard and Truffaut sought out American texts to adapt for the screen in *A bout de souffle* and *Tirez sur le pianiste* but why both directors structured their films around the counterpoint of different, and often incompatible, narrative genres and voices.

Godard's early films also give a poignant expression to French cultural anxiety in overlaying or dressing the female body in the colors of the national flag, creating a metaphorical nexus that links the representation of women, the state of France, and the prostitution of women in mass culture, underlining the idea that the cinema exploits the body politic at the same time as, and in the same way as, the body female, and reinforcing the notion that the national question is a question of cinema.[5] We find instances of this in *Pierrot le fou* where Anna Karina is called "Marianne," the female figure who, traditionally, signifies the French Republic; where the color scheme of her apartment and her clothes are *bleu-blanc-rouge* – blue bathrobe, white walls, red saucepan; and when, sitting in the boat, she is positioned against a French tricolor.

But the red and the blue also signify the blood and bruises of a fictionalized and aestheticized violence that, as Leutrat suggests, is now beginning to be real. It is clear that both Marianne and Ferdinand are inspired by popular culture, by slapstick routines, cartoon strips, and pulp fiction. When they beat up a garage attendant they use a gag derived from Laurel and Hardy; when hitching a ride their vade mecum is the comic strip *La Bande des Pieds nickelés;* and when they are short of money they perform a "mimodrame," or comic sketch, for an improvised audience. Exaggeration, simplification, two dimensionality and ellipsis, all of which are typical of the graphics and the narrative techniques of the comic strip, are brilliantly reworked in the film's use of flat planes of primary colors and highlighting of picaresque incident, so that the car accident is shown in all its gory detail and the dialogue also often imitates that of a cartoon strip – "shit, there's another one" *[merde, y en a encore un]* (A-S, 80; W, 45).[6]

Yet gradually these features take on a tragic dimension. Ferdinand's death is an absurd irony because at the last minute he cannot put out the touch paper of the dynamite, and his failure transmutes the pop art blue painted on his face into the somberly pessimistic shades of de Staël, Yves Klein, or Picasso.[7] The Vietnam sketch cannot represent the reality of the war that erupts into the film in a news report heard by Marianne and Ferdinand just as they are embarking on their romantic adventure, and in a newsreel seen by Ferdinand recounting the atrocities committed by the American army at Danang, both of which bring home the point Godard was to make more emphatically in *Loin du Viêtnam/Far from Vietnam* (1967), namely that this war was not some far-off colonial conflict but a tragedy that deeply affected the lives of men and women in France and for which they bore some responsibility. For Godard, as for many French people of his generation who were deeply scarred by the Algerian crisis of the 1950s, the question of imperialism – American or Soviet – was often as important as French domestic politics. The international dimension continued to influence most of the political films created by the Dziga Vertov group in the wake of May 1968, which explore the link between imperialism and the activity of filmmaking, between the power to represent and the politics of the image. But at the same time *Pierrot le fou* tentatively begins the process of reorientation toward domestic concerns that was to become fully apparent in the ironically entitled *Tout va bien,* which is primarily about the state of France, as well as in all Godard's films of the 1970s.

Thus by 1974 the long love affair with American popular fiction and popular cinema, which had sustained the New Wave and seems an endless source of creativity in *Pierrot le fou,* had definitively ended. The popular art forms that had been considered especially "American" and admired for their ludic dimension, their gaiety, and their inventiveness, were now "naturalized" and exploited for their political potential. Just as the state of France is inscribed on the body of women in the 1960s, so now a woman's body symbolizes the change. In 1967 the apotheosis of American influence was achieved in Roger Vadim's film version of Jean-Claude Forest's sci-fi erotic comic strip, *Barbarella,* which starred American actress Jane Fonda as robotic sex object. But by 1972, when Fonda returned to French film in *Tout va bien,* her role was that of an earnest, feminist journalist.

Naturalization or domestication took many forms. The *Série noire,* launched in 1945 to publish translations of American thrillers, had offered Godard and his contemporaries texts to adapt for the screen, but now started publishing original French material that found its way into the cinema. The highly political thrillers of Jean-Patrick Manchette were typical of this new mode, and Claude Chabrol's 1974 adaptation of Manchette's *Nada/The Nada Gang,* featuring a gang of post-1968 anarchist terrorists, marked the expression of these new concerns in cinema. Hollywood noted this shift as well and, in *The French Connection* (William Friedkin, 1971), relocated the mafia from Chicago and Los Angeles to Marseilles and Nice as did Jacques Deray (*Borsalino* [1969], *Borsalino & Co* [1974]) and Jean-Pierre Melville (*Le Samouraï/The Samurai* [1969], *Le Cercle rouge/The Red Circle* [1972]). Bertrand Tavernier, hitherto one of the most ardent proponents of American cinema in France, filmed Jim Thompson's thriller *Pop. 1280* as a virulent critique of French colonialism in *Coup de*

Torchon/Clean Slate (1981) and adapted the aesthetics of the western to a story of medieval France in *La Passion Béatrice/Beatrice*
(1987). The comic strip ceased to be nostalgic and sentimental like
La Bande des Pieds nickelés and turned to satirical politics with the
newspaper *Charlie Hebdo* and to sociology in Claire Bretécher's *Les
Frustrés*. The performance techniques of the "mimodrame" were
taken up by the political cabarets of the *café-théâtre* that flourished
in the early 1970s and were transposed into the cinema in the
films of Bertrand Blier (*Les Valseuses/Going Places* [1973], *Buffet
froid* [1979]), Patrice Leconte (*Les Bronzés* [1978]), and Jean-Marie
Poiré (*Le Père Noël est une ordure/Santa Claus Is a Louse* [1982]).[8]

THE DEATH OF THE *AUTEUR*

The process of disengagement from American culture is
also achieved by questioning the role of the filmmaker, of whom
two appear in *Pierrot le fou*. The American director, Samuel Fuller,
has a small role as one of the guests at Monsieur and Madame
Espresso's cocktail party. Regarded by *Cahiers du cinéma* as an
auteur, Fuller was known as a director of B movies that were
inspired by his background as a crime reporter and war correspon-
dent, and he had recently scored a critical success in France with
Shock Corridor (1963). In his brief appearance he defines cinema as
a battleground consisting of the formulaic juxtaposition of primitive human actions and feelings: "Love . . . Hate . . . Violence . . .
Death" (*A-S*, 75; *W*, 28). Toward the end of the film, Jean Seberg
appears in the fictional role of television reporter Patricia Leacock
on location in Marrakech in a clip from Godard's short film *Le
grand escroc* (1964). This pair typifies Godard's early style, the virtuoso combination of the B movie and the documentary to be
found in his first film, *A bout de souffle*.[9] Fuller, in Europe to film
Les Fleurs du mal, is like Fritz Lang in *Le Mépris* filming an adaptation of *The Odyssey* for a Hollywood producer. Patricia Leacock, in
contrast, shares a name with the celebrated American documentary director Richard Leacock and states that her work is *cinéma
vérité* like that of Jean Rouch.[10] In both instances the context pro-

vides an ironic challenge to the aesthetics of these filmmakers. The cocktail party scene is suffused with the glow of the colored filters that Godard had already used in *Le Mépris* and *Une Femme est une femme/A Woman Is a Woman* (1961) and that he would later use in the commercials sequence of *Tout va bien,* to suggest the exploitation of women's bodies by the consumer society, advertising, and Hollywood cinema. The Patricia Leacock sequence is positioned after the Vietnam newsreel and what she says reminds the audience that Rouch's films show how the influence of Hollywood penetrates into the deepest corners of Africa, transforming the imaginative framework of the local people and changing documentary into spectacle.[11]

These are only two of the many occasions when fictional or real filmmakers appear in Godard's films. *Pierrot le fou* belongs within the 1960s tradition that began to question authorship as a "transcendental source and guarantee of meaning" and that was given new impetus by May 1968, seen as the supreme revolt against de Gaulle, the symbolic father of the nation.[12] After May 1968 it became impossible for the filmmaker to remain an auteur in the sense that the New Wave had intended, and Godard was not alone in problematizing the notion in the aftermath of the Events. Like many other filmmakers, including Truffaut who had perhaps been an even more persuasive polemicist for auteur theory, he began to reexamine the metaphor by reinserting familial structures into his post-1968 films.

The New Wave's version of modernity focused on young people with no familial or generational ties, the petty bourgeois equivalents of the famous literary and artistic couples whose activities filled the newspapers and who sometimes ran them too: Louis Aragon and Elsa Triolet, Jean-Paul Sartre and Simone de Beauvoir, Jacques Servan-Schreiber and Françoise Giroud, Yves Montand and Simone Signoret.[13] In *Pierrot le fou* this couple is in extreme difficulties and continues to be so in Godard's later films, such as *Tout va bien* and *Numéro deux* (1975); while in *Sauve qui peut (la vie)* it has become comically dysfunctional. A glance at the work of Maurice Pialat, Jacques Doillon, or Philippe Garrel in the post-

1968 period confirms that the family had become a topic of central concern for many filmmakers.[14] Truffaut's elegiac *La Nuit américaine/Day for Night* (1973) harks back to a theme already evident in the films of the 1950s in which an analogy was often developed between the threat posed by modernization to the capitalist structure typical of France, namely the small family business, and the threat to the artisanal filmmaking typical of France, endangered by the big machines of Hollywood. Calling *La Nuit américaine* "the last film that will ever be made in this way," Truffaut casts himself as paterfamilias and godfather to the film crew and actors who are his extended family, as well as the proprietor of a family business. Godard always positions himself slightly obliquely in relation to familial structures, as the video watcher and manipulator in *Numéro deux*, the divorced father in *Sauve qui peut (la vie)*, the slightly ridiculous uncle in *Prénom Carmen/First Name Carmen* (1983). And, of course, he depicts paternity as problematic in *Je vous salue, Marie/Hail Mary* (1985). But he also gives the analogy a new twist by linking familial structures to questions of representation as well as to patriarchy.

By the end of the 1960s – in other words, a decade later than in comparable European countries such as Britain or Germany – television finally reached virtually all households in France only to find its influence sharply questioned as a consequence of May 1968, which revealed the medium's complicity with state power and its reluctance to present more than one point of view. The apparently innocent image, the transparent "window on the world," was revealed to be manipulated and distorted to support the government party. Godard's personal trajectory in the 1970s, his departure from Paris and creation of the Sonimage company, was an attempt to create a space in which he exercised sufficient control for the image to be as unmediated and unmanipulated by the forces of capitalism as it had been, hypothetically, in some utopian past. His video and television films of the 1970s, *Numéro deux* (1975), *Six fois deux/Sur et sous la communication* (1976), and *France/tour/détour/deux enfants* (1977–8) are, at first glance, very different from *Pierrot le fou* since they show an evident desire to engage with "ordinary" people and to place on screen individuals and groups previously excluded from representation. They are a far cry from *Pierrot le fou*'s concern with theatricality and performance and its occasional reminders to the spectator that it is a fiction film. Yet if we compare *Numéro deux* to its intertext, André Téchiné's *Souvenirs d'en France/French Provincial* from the same year, we can see that although the former imitates the look of a television documentary, and the latter a 1940s melodrama, they both link subjectivity and representation to the family romance and the history of France. The *auteur*, as theorized by the New Wave, has become a nostalgic fantasy of patriarchal control, so that he is distanced from the real family matters in *Numéro deux* by the framing devices, and he is feminized or infantilized in *Souvenirs d'en France* by the powerful women whose subjectivity dominates the narrative and who take on the role of "heroes" of the romance.

TU PEUX PAS DIRE BALZAC? ("CAN'T YOU SAY BALZAC?")

But the legacy of realist fiction to the cinema was already at issue in *Pierrot le fou*, as it is, indirectly, in many of Godard's earlier films. His first feature, *A bout de souffle*, interweaves two fictional genres, the thriller and the love story, in such a way that each comments on and becomes imbricated with the other. *Le Mépris* is an encounter between a founding text of European literature, the Hollywood adaptation of it, and a modern love story. *Pierrot le fou* provides an even more complex set of intertextual relations and an exploration of a whole range of fictional modes.[15] The issues are summed up in Ferdinand's ironic comment on the shift from telephone exchanges designated by names, such as "Balzac," to exchanges designated by numbers (*A-S*, 74; W, 27), a comment repeated when he telephones home just before killing himself and says to the operator, "Have *you* forgotten who Balzac is too?" [*Vous aussi, vous avez oublié qui est Balzac?*] (*A-S*, 108; cf. W, 103).[16]

For the proponents of the *nouveau roman*, the nineteenth-century novelist served as an exemplar of classic realist fiction, the fictional mode they attempted to overcome in a different approach to realism, often based on a playful use of alternative narrative genres such as the detective story.[17] In the same way, *Pierrot le fou* forgets or ignores Balzac by mixing a range of different fictions and a range of narrative genres and modes – the thriller *(série noire)*, comic strip *(bande dessinée)*, *cinéroman*, journal, news clip *(faits divers)*, adventure story, autobiography, prose poem – which are often associated with different linguistic registers – advertising slogans, poetry, songs, journalism – to create a profoundly dialogic text.

The film is an adaptation of Lionel White's novel *Obsession* (1962), translated into French the following year as *Le Démon d'onze heures*[18] and one of six White novels to be published in the *Série noire* collection in the early 1960s. It contains many of the ingredients considered, at least in France, to be typical of the genre: first-person narrative, reinvention of identity, flight across America, a femme fatale, with the added twist, in this instance, that she is a girl of seventeen. One piece of dialogue in the novel echoes in reverse form the celebrated exchange about William Faulkner in *A bout de souffle* and may have initially attracted Godard because of its transcultural implications: "You know," says the narrator Conrad Madden to Allie the baby-sitter, "I'm beginning to feel like a character in a Françoise Sagan novel." "I don't read much," she replies.[19]

It is often said that the film bears little relation to the novel. In fact, although the setting is obviously transposed from America to France, much of the detail is the same: the unemployed advertising executive of the American novel becomes the unemployed TV executive of the French film, but his acquaintances all work in advertising; the realization that the baby-sitter has committed a violent murder, the search for her gangster brother, and the reference to her relationship with Frank, Ferdinand's friend, are all taken from the novel. What is more, like the eighteenth-century authors Godard admired, *Obsession* asks what is the status of truth in a text: "Allie, beyond question, is a congenital liar."[20] It also sees identity as a matter of performance: Conrad feels he has assumed the features of a Sagan character and he also gives Allie a makeover, teaching her to play the part of the middle-class housewife rather than the bored teenager of their first meeting. This topos is evident in Godard's films from the beginning: Michel Poiccard in *A bout de souffle* modeled himself on Humphrey Bogart; Angéla in *Une Femme est une femme* dreamed of being in a Hollywood musical "with Cyd Charisse." It is echoed in the musical and beach dance sequences in *Pierrot le fou* and referred to, with variations, in many later films.

Pierrot also draws strongly on the *bande dessinée*. We first see Ferdinand, whose literary tastes become an extremely important feature in the film, browsing in a bookshop next to the Jardin du Luxembourg in Paris. In another reference to eighteenth-century literature, the shop is called *Le Meilleur des Mondes* (the best of all worlds), and he is holding a copy of *La Bande des Pieds nickelés* that recounts the picaresque and comic adventures of the gangsters Ribouldingue, Croquignol, and Filochard in their travels across France.[21] From time to time either Ferdinand or Marianne is seen reading this album and, occasionally, an image from it is inserted as a close-up on screen. Later, when the couple has arrived on their improvised desert island, the paradisaical "best of all worlds," Ferdinand reads from Céline's *Guignol's Band*, a picaresque and burlesque account of the First World War as a puppet show or extended comic strip. The film's many other sources of textual material, like these examples, initially stage an encounter between "high" and "low" culture that divides along gender lines, so that when Ferdinand and Marianne imagine what they might have done with the money, she says they could have gone to "Chicago, Las Vegas, Monte Carlo"; he prefers "Florence, Venice, Athens" (*A-S*, 84; W, 51). It is as though Ferdinand, the reader of Élie Faure's *Histoire de l'art* and of Defoe, Verne, and Conrad (whose name is echoed in that of the protagonist of *Obsession*), as well as Voltaire, Diderot, and Prévost, had imitated Céline and chosen to rework the eighteenth-century picaresque and the nineteenth-century adventure tale in a twentieth-century mode when he ran off with Marianne, living according to the morality and sexual politics of film noir in which the woman urges the more passive man – as in

Reading companions

Manon Lescaut or in *Bonnie and Clyde* (Arthur Penn, 1967) – to commit more and more atrocious and sexually exciting crimes.

These experiments with gender-based cultural preferences and assumptions bore fruit after 1968 in the strong French comic tradition, led by Bertrand Blier and Josiane Balasko, whose films exploit the comic potential of actors or characters who do not behave according to physical type (*Tenue de soirée/Ménage* [1986], *Trop belle pour toi/Too Beautiful for You* [1989], *Sac de nœuds* [1985]). They have also encouraged a critical tradition according to which this juxtaposition of textual sources is an examination of Ferdinand's subjectivity, exemplified in Ferdinand's remark, *"Y a pas d'unité. Je devrais avoir l'impression d'être unique, j'ai l'impression d'être plusieurs"* ("There's no unity. I should feel I am unique, I

High vs. low culture

have the feeling of being many") (*A-S*, 75; cf. W, 34). This has also meant that the narrative is viewed as "discontinuous" or "deconstructed" and that the film is usually described as a "montage" or a "collage" of disparate elements.[22]

Although the film is all these things, its structure is more accurately described as a palimpsest – that is to say, a work in which texts are written over other texts in such a way that glimpses of earlier texts interact with new ones. The characters, therefore, operate the kind of fictional "world switch" that critics have identified in the writings of Raymond Queneau, whose *Pierrot mon ami* is a major intertext of the film.[23] The film creates the extraordinary sensation that Marianne and Ferdinand are observing themselves perform as fictional characters, that they are simultaneously the authors and narrators of, as well as characters in, particular kinds of fictions. It relies on verbal and visual indicators to designate such switches as well as innumerable references to the differences between life and fiction. Very early, when Ferdinand and Marianne have just decided to abscond, Marianne asks whether their "adventure"[24] can be as satisfying as that in a fiction: "What makes me sad is that life and the novel are so very different . . . I would like them to be the same . . . clear . . . logical . . . organized. . . . But they aren't like that at all" [ce qui me rend triste, c'est que la vie et le roman c'est différent. . . . Je voudrais que ce soit pareil . . . clair, . . . logique, . . . organisé, . . . mais ça ne l'est pas] (A-S, 76; cf. W, 36), and it is immediately following this remark that she first calls Ferdinand by the fictional name of Pierrot she has invented for him. The characters attempt to impose a "novelistic" structure on their adventure by a rational division of their experiences into "chapters" that, as has frequently been pointed out, do not succeed one another in numerical order: "next chapter," "chapter eight," "chapter seven." Sometimes they give the chapter a title, as in "a season in hell" [une saison en enfer].[25] Frequently, the contents are spoken before they are shown, so that a world switch is usually accompanied by a voice or voices off: "Marianne told . . . a complicated story" [Marianne raconta . . . une histoire . . . compliquée] (A-S, 79; cf. W, 40–2). Here the past historic tense (raconta), conventionally used in French to indicate the narrative mode,[26] is used to take the couple outside the first-person narrative of the thriller. In the 1950s and 1960s, the use of this tense had been identified and challenged by Barthes and by the nouveaux romanciers as the means by which the illusion of a stable, coherent, and bourgeois world of fiction was created.[27] Thus when a writer deliberately chooses not to use the past historic in a narrative, as is the case in Camus's L'Étranger (The Outsider), the effect is immensely disturbing.[28] In the same way, when the past historic tense is used in film in which the immediacy of the action would appear to preclude narrative distance, a similar disorientation occurs. In Pierrot le fou the past historic is used as a marker on a number of key occasions (A-S, 79, 80, 82, 84, 86), and it is often

"A complicated story"

accompanied by linguistic references that prepare for an impend-
ing world switch: "Waking from a bad dream" [Sortir d'un mauvais
rêve]; "It was the right moment to get away from this stinking,
lousy world" [C'était le moment de quitter ce monde dégueulasse et
pourri]; "the following day" [le lendemain]; and, even more explicitly, "it was an adventure film" [c'était un film d'aventures], "it was a
love story" [c'était un roman d'amour] (A-S, 79–80; W, 44–7). Marianne even wishes to precipitate the switch: "We've finished the
Jules Verne novel. Now we're going back to where we started in a
thriller with cars, guns, and night clubs" (A-S, 90; cf. W, 69). Many
of their stories are not original but are "pinched from books," like
the stories of heroism, death, and the macabre they recount to
raise money in the café, stories about Aucassin and Nicolette or

the aviation hero Guynemer. On other occasions, the switch is designated by visual effects as when Ferdinand and Marianne disguise themselves as the nephew of Uncle Sam and the niece of Uncle Ho, or when visual inserts from *La Bande des Pieds nickelés* are used to suggest the kind of story world they happen to be in.

The fragmentary nature of these stories, the mixture of genres, and the complexity of the intertextual references all render *Pierrot le fou* a postmodern film before postmodernism was invented, but this does not make it inconsequential, as many of its first reviewers thought. Godard's text is a brilliantly controlled exploration of different narrative genres. On occasions it appears playfully nostalgic for the satisfying narratives of classic realist fiction; at other times it appears to experiment with autobiography in its depiction of the disintegration of the Karina/Godard marriage.

The palimpsest structure allows the film to be more than one thing at the same time and to superimpose different times and different moods by varying the tenses and mood of the verb and by using the voice *off*, which introduces a different time structure and disrupts or breaks into the continuous present of the film. In *A bout de souffle* Godard had experimented, in a fairly restrained manner, with the dissociation of sound and image, using the possibilities of post-synchronization to achieve narrative ellipsis and a sense of rapidity. These experiments develop in *Pierrot le fou* into a thoroughgoing reflexion on narrative. Technical resources are linked to a play with grammatical structures, so that the voice *off* speaks a different tense, often the past historic, from the continuous present of the film, the infinitive is used to predict actions that will not be seen, and the present tense is used performatively to indicate an action that is not shown: "I am placing my hand on your knee" *[Je mets ma main sur ton genou]* (A-S, 88; cf. W, 37).[29]

Much of Godard's later work pursues these possibilities. *Numéro deux* and *Six fois deux*, for example, exploit the technological resources of video communication to this end. The filmmaker in *Numéro deux* is able to mix images in the same way as sound is mixed so as to hold in view two images simultaneously and to create a third that synthesizes the two. In this way the version of the

Hegelian synthesis propounded by the central character Sandrine is also represented visually. In *Six fois deux* he can overwrite the sound track using a character generator to print on the screen comments that reinforce or contradict what is being said. Film is less technically amenable to this kind of experimentation than video is. Nevertheless, in *Passion* Godard achieves extreme disjunctions of sound and image and gives the sound track a high degree of autonomy by, for example, interrupting lyrical musical sequences in mid-crescendo leaving the viewer/listener profoundly dissatisfied, drowning speech in traffic noise, or, in a radically desynchronizing move, showing a person speaking while playing a sound track that does not correspond to what is being said. Many independent filmmakers in the 1970s experimented in this way with assonance and dissonance, anachrony and synchrony, but only Marguerite Duras most clearly perceived the radical possibilities of these ideas. In *Son Nom de Venise dans Calcutta désert* (1976) she reused the sound track of *India Song* (1975), but her images were of an empty landscape, so she created long sequences of compelling beauty that have no narrative function like the shots of the sky in *Pierrot le fou* or *Passion*.

POETRY AND PAINTING

One of the most poignant scenes in *Pierrot le fou* takes place on the beach of the "desert island" retreat. This is the moment when Marianne says "of course" she will not leave Ferdinand, and we know that "of course" she will. Their adventure disintegrates thereafter, the narrative becomes more difficult to follow, and it ends in the death of both parties, making sense of the film's frequent references to doomed romantic couples, especially those who encountered their nemesis in a distant paradise or a foreign land – Aucassin and Nicolette, Paul and Virginie, Ferdinand and Virginia (in *Guignol's Band*), or Verlaine and Rimbaud. This is the moment when sexual stereotyping is most obvious, and we realize that they have not "reinvented love." But it is also at this point that Ferdinand assumes an authorial role and begins

writing his diary, like Robinson Crusoe. That text appears fragmentary because it is seen in close-up, but we can nevertheless
just detect the quotation from Valéry: "poetic language rises from
the ruins" *[le langage poétique surgit des ruines]* (*A-S*, 88; W, 59).

Ferdinand's diary or journal makes sense of the sequence of references to Rimbaud in the film. We are told that one of the "chapters" is, as mentioned earlier, *une saison en enfer* after the title Rimbaud gave his great poem, itself a mixture of genres, some prose,
some verse, and a transposed account of his flight with Verlaine,
"*la vierge folle.*" The section entitled *L'Alchimie du verbe* ("Alchemy
of the Word") sets out the kind of material, the "ruins" from
which Rimbaud created his poetic language. He writes that he
"found laughable the celebrated names of painting and modern
poetry" and "I liked stupid paintings, door panels, stage sets, back-
drops for acrobats, signs, popular engravings, old-fashioned literature, church Latin, erotic books with bad spelling, novels of our
grandmothers, books from childhood, old operas, ridiculous
refrains, naive rhythms."[30] From this very fragmentary, disparate,
and, above all, popular material came the "alchemy" that allowed
Rimbaud to invent a new poetic language using the "synaesthe-
sia" (correspondence of sensations) for which he, like Baudelaire,
is celebrated: "I invented the color of the vowels – A black, E
white, I red, O blue, U green – I regulated the form and movement
of each consonant, and, with instinctive rhythms, I flattered
myself that I had invented a poetic language accessible some day
to all the senses."[31]

This passage, extraordinarily well known in the history of
French literature as a manifesto of the new poetics, shows us the
breadth of Godard's ambition in *Pierrot le fou* and allows us to consider the explosions of color, when a custard pie is transformed
into a fireworks display or when the lights from the road play on
the windshield as Ferdinand and Marianne drive away from the
cocktail party, as *mises en abyme*, miniature examples of the transformation of cinematic language into poetry.[32] The "unity" Ferdinand seeks is one of art rather than subjectivity, a means to syn-
thesize the multiple resonances of language and of color.

The last words of the film are a quotation from Rimbaud's poem "L'Éternité": *Elle est retrouvée // - Quoi? - L'Éternité. // C'est la mer allée // Avec le soleil.*[33] The first word spoken is the name of the great seventeenth-century Spanish painter Velázquez. Ferdinand is reading aloud from Élie Faure's *Histoire de l'art* in which Velázquez is described both as "the painter of evenings, spaces and silence" and as the pitiless chronicler of the corruption and decadence of the Spanish court under Philip IV: "The world he lived in was sad. A degenerate king, inbred infantas, idiots, dwarfs, cripples, a few deformed clowns clothed as princes" *[Le monde où il vivait était triste. Un roi dégénéré, des enfants malades, des idiots, des nains, des informes, quelques pitres monstrueux vêtus en princes]* (A-S, 72; cf. W, 24). Then Ferdinand emerges from the bathtub in which he was reading and reluctantly accompanies his wife to a cocktail party thrown by her parents, peopled by figures as grotesque as those at the Spanish court and, disgusted with this charade, he takes off with the baby-sitter Marianne to embark on the adventures that form the action of the film and lead, ultimately, to his suicide.

Godard's films are studded with visual and verbal references to the arts, especially to painting, and his films often "quote" portraits of women, or "represent" women, such as Joan of Arc, Mary, or Carmen, as well as film stars, who have become icons as a result of a long figurative or cinematic tradition. Frequently, the reproduction of a well-known painting, pinned to the wall, is compared to the filmic "portrait" of the actress starring in the film. This is evident in the comparisons established in *A bout de souffle* between Jean Seberg and portraits by Renoir and Modigliani, and in *Vivre sa vie/My Life to Live* (1962) in which a shot of Anna Karina's head is juxtaposed with a clip of that of Falconetti playing Saint Joan in Carl Dreyer's *La Passion de Jeanne d'Arc/The Passion of Joan of Arc* (1928) and with a photograph of Elizabeth Taylor while Godard's voice reads from Poe's story *The Oval Portrait*.

Nevertheless, the reference to Velázquez signals a new departure. Hitherto Godard's preferred artists have been masters of the modern tradition in painting, such as Renoir, Picasso, or Modigliani – painters whose attention is concentrated on the surface of the canvas and planes of color, as with Renoir and the fauves, or on the exploration of form, as with Picasso and the cubists. In *Pierrot le fou* these artists are no longer interpreted as modernists but as representatives of a national tradition, evident in the association of the name of Renoir with that of Marianne. It is Picasso's Spanish origins and nationalist sentiments that are evoked rather than his contribution to modernism, and the quotation of his painting *Pierrot au masque* links Ferdinand to the project of reinventing an identity and compares him to the *pitres* (clowns) of Velázquez. More generally, the reference to Velázquez signals a shift in interest from Italy to Spain. In *A bout de souffle* and *Le Mépris*, Italy represented the mythical locus of late 1950s modernity: Rome was the city to which Michel wished to transport Patricia, and the home of Cinecittà Studios where much of *Le Mépris* takes place. In *Pierrot le fou* Ferdinand and Marianne also contemplate fleeing to Italy although, like Michel and Patricia, they never get there. By contrast, Spain represents the weight of history and, perhaps, the failure of the modern (Franco did not die until 1975), and Ferdinand, whose name echoes that of so many of the kings of Spain and who is a former teacher of Spanish at the Lycée St. Louis, abandons his Italian wife and her parents for an imaginary return to the sources of a different kind of art, away from a modern world that has become corrupt.

The reference to Velázquez sets the tone for the entire film and indicates that *Pierrot le fou* marks the start of a move from an aesthetic of surfaces to one of depth, from planes to spaces. Gilles Deleuze demonstrated how, very frequently, *nouvelle vague* protagonists appear physically – and perhaps psychologically – two dimensional, positioned against flat surfaces rather than located in space.[34] This is especially true of Godard, whose films up to and including *Tout va bien* contain a series of flamboyant and justly famous lateral pans, which, given their context, must be interpreted as critiques of the "lack of depth" of modern society: *Vivre sa vie* shows the prostitutes lined up against a graffiti-covered wall, *Week-end* (1967) shows an immensely long traffic jam, *Tout va bien* shows both the cross section of the factory and the raid on the supermarket. Not surprisingly, in *Pierrot le fou,* it is the cocktail party that is filmed in this manner with the camera following Ferdinand laterally as he passes from group to group catching snatches of conversations almost entirely made up of advertising slogans delivered deadpan.

Pierrot le fou begins the critique of the visual regime that Godard had helped to create, and uses Velázquez to bring into play a different tradition and a different view of corruption. Instead of the harsh, artificial lighting of the colored filters, he paints twilights and evenings; instead of the noisy chatter of advertising executives, he paints silence; and above all, instead of the surfaces of the modernists, he attempts to represent depth.[35] The lateral pan disappears as the film progresses to make way for the majestic, slowly rising shot of the sky to the accompaniment of lyrical music.

Painterliness of this kind disappeared from Godard's work until the end of the 1970s when *Sauve qui peut (la vie)* marked his return to mainstream filmmaking. Even though that film echoes the formalism of the 1960s in its division into sections with titles, it parodies the themes of that decade: prostitution comes to be represented by an overdressed and heavily made-up woman in high heels walking down a country lane past a field of cows; advertising is represented by the incongruous arrival in a village square of a Formula One racing car painted in the colors of Marlboro cigarettes; communications technology, in which Godard's Sonimage Company had invested its hopes for a democratization of access to the media, is parodied in an orgy staged as a feedback loop. In the same way, the primary colors and flat planes of the earlier films, evident as we have seen in parts but not all of *Pierrot le fou,* are replaced by greens, yellows, and pastels, and the freeze frame technique developed in the television series *France/tour/détour* is used to break down color so that the image begins to resemble that of a *pointilliste* painting. In *Sauve qui peut (la vie)* the viewer has the distinct impression that Godard has rediscovered the natural world: the poetically named Denise Rimbaud is leaving her job in television to live in the country, a move that brings with it new compositional possibilities based on landscape and vegetation; and many of Godard's subsequent films celebrate nature, above all, perhaps, *Nouvelle vague/New Wave* (1990), which is a sensuous record of the changing colors of the trees, the rippling of water on a lake, or the intriguing patterns of mountains and valleys. For Godard, as for many of his contemporaries, the combined influence of May 1968 and the oil crisis of 1973 challenged the virtues of unchecked modernization, encouraging the search for an alternative aesthetic in a new pastoralism.

PAST HISTORIC

The first encounter between Ferdinand and Marianne is said to have taken place four or five years before the action of the film, and an unspecified period of time elapses between their flight from Paris and the final sequences when they part and meet up again. Even so, like many New Wave films, *Pierrot le fou* almost entirely lacks a historical dimension or a strong teleological movement. In a manner typical of the 1960s, the action takes place in some unspecified present with only the intermittent references to Vietnam to remind us of the world outside that of the diegesis. There is no future tense: the love between Ferdinand and Marianne is "without a future" *[sans lendemain]* and their actions a series of superimposed presents. This has remained true of Godard's cinema, so that although he is extraordinarily attentive to current trends and fashions, particularly those of a cultural kind, he did not participate in the desire to rediscover or rewrite history that was so critical in the wake of 1968. The revisionism that became possible after the death of de Gaulle transformed documentary filmmaking, as seen in Marcel Ophuls's *Le Chagrin et la pitié/The Sorrow and the Pity* (1970), as well as fiction films, such as Louis Malle's *Lacombe Lucien* (1974), but it did not engage Godard. Instead, the key text in *Pierrot le fou,* with respect to Godard's later cinema, is Élie Faure's *Histoire de l'art* because, for Godard, art is history. He has explained this by saying, "When you get older, you become more interested in decisive moments."[36] The palimpsest

narrative developed in *Pierrot le fou* enables Godard to view history
not as the "total resurrection of the past," which is the ambition
of the heritage film with its investment in authenticity, but as
a continuous present kept alive by iconography, a kind of *musée
imaginaire.*

Pierrot le fou directly prefigures two films of the 1980s. The first
is *Prénom Carmen* (1983), which, as Laura Mulvey has pointed out,
is similarly a story of a doomed romantic couple.[37] The other is
Passion, whose title manifestly takes up Samuel Fuller's definition
of the cinema as "emotion." There are various narratives in *Passion,* but the most spectacular concerns the filmmaker Jerzy's
attempts to stage and film history paintings by Rembrandt, Goya,
and Delacroix to the accompaniment of snatches of Mozart's
Requiem. These extraordinary tableaux are like the frozen frames of
Sauve qui peut (la vie) or the inserts of *La Bande des Pieds nickelés* in
Pierrot le fou, moments when, thanks to the cinema, the present is
overlaid by the past historic.

NOTES

1. Terminology developed by Gilles Deleuze in his *Cinema 1: The
   Movement-Image,* trans. Hugh Tomlinson and Barbara Habberjam
   (Minneapolis: University of Minnesota Press, 1986), and *Cinema 2:
   The Time-Image,* trans. Hugh Tomlinson and Robert Galeta (Minneapolis: University of Minnesota Press, 1989) (*Cinéma 1. L'Image-
   Mouvement* and *Cinéma 2. L'Image-Temps* [Paris: Éditions de Minuit,
   1983, 1985]).
2. Jacques Becker's tale of rival gangs in *Touchez pas au grisbi/Grisbi*
   (1954) is a good example of the way cinema addressed the question
   of "Americanization," a topic discussed in Pascal Quignard's novel,
   significantly entitled *L'Occupation américaine* (Paris: Éditions du
   Seuil, 1994). The history of French attitudes toward America is usefully traced in Michel Winock, *Nationalisme, antisémitisme et fas-
   cisme en France* (Paris: Éditions du Seuil, 1982), 50–76.
3. See, for example, his "Défense et illustration du découpage clas-
   sique," B, 80–4; N&M, 26–30.
4. Cf. Harold Bloom, *The Anxiety of Influence: A Theory of Poetry* (New
   York: Oxford University Press, 1973).
5. Cf. discussion by Jean-Louis Leutrat in this volume.
6. This is brilliantly discussed by Barthélemy Amengual in Michel
   Estève and Barthélemy Amengual (eds.), "Jean-Luc Godard – Au-delà

du récit," *Études cinématographiques* 57/61 (1967): especially 149 and 153.

7. The suicide of Nicolas de Staël in 1955 transformed him into a contemporary art legend; Yves Klein, known for his body art, painted blues exclusively around the end of the 1950s; Picasso's "blue period" was marked by deep social pessimism.

8. For more detailed discussion of the relationship between *café-théâtre* and cinema, see Jill Forbes, *The Cinema in France: After the New Wave* (London: Macmillan, 1992), 172–9.

9. The film was dedicated to Monogram Pictures and starred Jean Seberg.

10. See *L'Avant-Scène Cinéma*, 46 (1965): 39: "Inspector: 'You make documentary films like Mr Rouch?' Patricia: 'That's right. It's truth motion picture [sic] le cinéma vérité.'"

11. *Le soin de chercher à quel moment on avait abandonné le personnage fictif pour reprendre le vrai, si tant est qu'il existât* ("carefully looking for . . . that moment when one abandons the fictional character in order to discover the true one . . . if such a thing exists" [*A-S*, 98; W, 83]). This recalls the scenes in Rouch's *Les Maîtres fous* (1955) when the Africans become performers who interact in the roles of Hollywood film stars like Dorothy Lamour.

12. The "death of the author" is usefully discussed by Michael Worton in Jill Forbes and Michael Kelly (eds.), *French Cultural Studies* (Oxford: Oxford University Press, 1995), 191–3.

13. Famous and fictional couples are illuminatingly discussed by Kristin Ross, *Fast Cars, Clean Bodies* (Cambridge, MA: MIT Press, 1995), 123–56.

14. Doillon even made a film called *La Vie de famille* in 1985. For further discussion, see Forbes, *The Cinema in France: After the New Wave*, 200–30.

15. Many of these are explored in T. Jefferson Kline's fascinating essay "The ABC of Godard's Quotations" in his *Screening the Text: Intertextuality in New Wave French Cinema* (Baltimore: Johns Hopkins University Press, 1992), 184–221.

16. So called after the Rue de Balzac, and designating the area near the Champs-Élysées where film production companies usually had their offices.

17. Alain Robbe-Grillet published his *For a New Novel,* trans. Richard Howard (New York: Grove Press, 1965) in 1963 (*Pour un nouveau roman* [Paris: Gallimard]). In it he attacks "the only conception of the novel to have currency today . . . that of Balzac" (15).

18. Lionel White, *Le Démon d'onze heures* [sic], traduit de l'américain par Bernard Robillon (Paris: Gallimard, 1963).

19. Lionel White, *Obsession* (London: T. V. Boardman & Co., 1962), 25. Recall Jean Seberg starred in the film version of Françoise Sagan's *Bonjour Tristesse* directed by Otto Preminger in 1958.

20. Ibid., 47.
21. This long-running cartoon series, first published in 1908, was drawn by René Pellos in the period 1948 to 1979.
22. Amengual was the best exponent of the "discontinuity" thesis in the 1960s; Kline of the "deconstructed narrative" in the 1990s.
23. I am indebted to Teresa Bridgeman for this terminology. Amengual, "Jean-Luc Godard – Au-delà du récit" discusses Godard's debt to Queneau without identifying this process.
24. The term *aventure* is ambiguous in French, meaning both adventure and love affair.
25. This title is, of course, borrowed from Arthur Rimbaud's great poem *Une Saison en enfer.* I return to this matter later.
26. Cf. Émile Benveniste, "The Correlations of Tense in the French Verb," in *Problems in General Linguistics,* trans. Mary Elizabeth Meek (Coral Gables: University of Miami Press, 1971), 205–15. Benveniste's essay was first published in 1959.
27. Cf. Roland Barthes, "Writing and the Novel," in *Writing Degree Zero,* trans. Annette Lavers and Colin Smith (London: Jonathan Cape, 1967), 26–34 (French text first published in 1953); Alain Robbe-Grillet, *For a New Novel,* 32: "All the technical elements of the narrative – systematic use of the past [historic] tense and the third person, unconditional adoption of a chronological development, linear plots, regular trajectory of passions . . . everything tended to impose the image of a stable, coherent, continuous, unequivocal, entirely decipherable universe."
28. This instance is discussed by Jean-Paul Sartre, "Camus' *The Outsider,*" in his *Literary and Philosophical Essays,* trans. Annette Michelson (London: Hutchinson, 1955), 38–9, and Benveniste, *Problems in General Linguistics,* 309 n. 13.
29. This is particularly true of the early flight sequences.
30. *Rimbaud, Complete Works, Selected Letters,* trans. Wallace Fowlie (Chicago: University of Chicago Press, 1966), 192–3:

    Je trouvais dérisoires les célébrités de la peinture et de la poésie moderne. . . . J'aimais les peintures idiotes, dessus de portes, décors, toiles de saltimbanques, enseignes, enluminures populaires, la littérature démodée, latin d'église, livres érotiques sans orthographe, romans de nos aïeules, contes de fées, petits livres d'enfance, opéras vieux, refrains niais, rythmes naïfs.

    Recall that both Jean Eustache, *Mes Petites amoureuses/My Little Loves* (1975), and Léos Carax, *Mauvais sang/Bad Blood* (1986), use references to *Une Saison en enfer* in the titles of their films.
31. Ibid., translation modified *[J'inventai la couleur des voyelles – A noir, E blanc, I rouge, O bleu, U vert – Je réglai la forme et le mouvement de chaque consonne, et, avec des rythmes instinctifs, je me flattai d'inventer un verbe poétique accessible, un jour ou l'autre, à tous les sens].* See also the poem entitled "Voyelles" referred to by Tom Conley.
32. In retrospect, Michel's facial contortions, imitated by Patricia in

A bout de souffle, look like a practice run for articulating Rimbaud's vowels, while the carefully orchestrated exclamations of "pleasure" in the orgy sequence of *Sauve qui peut (la vie)* might be read as a parody of "Voyelles."

33. Rimbaud, 138–9: "It has been found again // What has? – *Eternity* // It is the sea gone off // With the sun." Rimbaud uses or reuses these two lines in *Une Saison en enfer* in a slightly different version: *C'est la mer mêlée // Au soleil* (198–9). I am grateful to Michael Freeman for pointing this out.

34. See, for example, Gilles Deleuze, *Cinema 2: The Time-Image,* 189–203.

35. It is interesting that Michel Foucault's *Les Mots et les choses* (Paris: Gallimard, 1966) (*The Order of Things* [New York: Random House, 1970]), which begins with an analysis of the use of space in Velázquez's famous painting of the Infanta at the Spanish court, *Las Meninas,* was published a year after *Pierrot le fou* was first released. See the discussion by Tom Conley in this volume.

36. *CinémAction,* 52 (1989): 89, my translation.

37. Laura Mulvey, *Fetishism and Curiosity* (London: BFI, 1996), 90.

Filmography

The principal sources for this information are Bellour and Bandy (eds.), *Jean-Luc Godard: Son + Image 1974–1991;* Dixon, *The Films of Jean-Luc Godard;* and Douin, *Jean-Luc Godard.* Additional information through 1976 is available in Lesage, *Jean-Luc Godard: A Guide to References and Resources.* English-language titles are those most commonly used to refer to the film, and may be either American or British.

1954

Opération Béton

Production	Jean-Luc Godard
Production Company	Actua Films
Direction	Jean-Luc Godard
Screenplay	Jean-Luc Godard
Cinematography	Adrien Porchet
Editing	Jean-Luc Godard
Music	Handel, Bach
Format/Duration	B/W, 35mm/17 min.

1955

Une Femme coquette

Production	Jean-Luc Godard
Production Company	Jean-Luc Godard
Direction	Jean-Luc Godard
Screenplay	Hans Lucas (pseudonym for Godard); from "Le Signe" by Guy de Maupassant

Cinematography	Hans Lucas
Editing	Hans Lucas
Music	Bach
Cast	Marie Lysandre, Roland Tolma, Jean-Luc Godard
Format/Duration	B/W, 16mm/10 min.

1957

Tous les garçons s'appellent Patrick (Charlotte et Véronique) / All Boys Are Called Patrick

Production	Pierre Braunberger
Production Company	Les Films de la Pléïade
Direction	Jean-Luc Godard
Screenplay	Eric Rohmer
Cinematography	Michel Latouche
Editing	Cécile Decugis
Music	Beethoven, Pierre Monsigny
Cast	Jean-Claude Brialy, Anne Colette, Nicole Berger
Format/Duration	B/W, 35mm/21 min.

1958

Une Histoire d'eau

Production	Pierre Braunberger
Production Company	Les Films de la Pléïade
Direction	Jean-Luc Godard, François Truffaut
Screenplay	François Truffaut
Cinematography	Michel Latouche
Editing	Jean-Luc Godard
Sound	Jacques Maumont
Cast	Jean-Claude Brialy, Caroline Dim, Jean-Luc Godard
Format/Duration	B/W, 35mm/18 min.

1959

Charlotte et son jules

Production	Pierre Braunberger
Production Company	Les Films de la Pléïade
Direction	Jean-Luc Godard
Screenplay	Jean-Luc Godard
Cinematography	Michel Latouche
Editing	Cécile Decugis
Sound	Jacques Maumont
Music	Pierre Monsigny
Cast	Jean-Paul Belmondo, Anne Colette, Gérard Blain
Format/Duration	B/W, 35mm/20 min.

1960

A bout de souffle / Breathless

Production	Georges de Beauregard
Production Company	Société Nouvelle de Cinéma
Direction	Jean-Luc Godard
Screenplay	Jean-Luc Godard; idea by François Truffaut
Cinematography	Raoul Coutard
Editing	Cécile Decugis, Lila Herman
Sound	Jacques Maumont
Music	Martial Solal, Mozart
Cast	Jean-Paul Belmondo, Jean Seberg, Henri-Jacques Huet, Daniel Boulanger
Format/Duration	B/W, 35mm/90 min.

Le Petit soldat (released 1963)

Production	Georges de Beauregard
Production Company	Société Nouvelle de Cinéma
Direction	Jean-Luc Godard
Screenplay	Jean-Luc Godard

Cinematography	Raoul Coutard
Editing	Agnès Guillemot, Nadine Marquand, Lila Herman
Sound	Jacques Maumont
Music	Pierre Monsigny
Cast	Michel Subor, Anna Karina, Henri-Jacques Huet, Paul Beauvais
Format/Duration	B/W, 35mm/88 min.

1961

Une Femme est une femme / *A Woman Is a Woman*

Production	Georges de Beauregard, Carlo Ponti
Production Company	Rome-Paris Films/Unidex, Euro International
Direction	Jean-Luc Godard
Screenplay	Jean-Luc Godard; idea by Geneviève Cluny
Cinematography	Raoul Coutard
Editing	Agnès Guillemot, Lila Herman
Sound	Guy Villette
Music	Michel Legrand
Cast	Anna Karina, Jean-Paul Belmondo, Jean-Claude Brialy, Marie Dubois
Format/Duration	Color, 35mm/84 min.

"La Paresse" (contribution to *Les Sept péchés capitaux*) / "Sloth" in *The Seven Capital Sins*

Production Company	Les Films Gibé/Franco-London Films/Titanus
Direction	Jean-Luc Godard
Screenplay	Jean-Luc Godard
Cinematography	Henri Decaë
Editing	Jacques Gaillard
Sound	Jean-Claude Marchetti, Jean Labussière
Music	Michel Legrand
Cast	Eddie Constantine, Nicole Mirel
Format/Duration	B/W, 35mm/15 min.

1962

Vivre sa vie / My Life to Live

Production	Pierre Braunberger
Production Company	Les Films de la Pléïade
Direction	Jean-Luc Godard
Screenplay	Jean-Luc Godard; documentation from *Où en est la prostitution?* by Marcel Sacotte
Cinematography	Raoul Coutard
Editing	Agnès Guillemot, Lila Lakshmanan
Sound	Guy Villette, Jacques Maumont
Music	Michel Legrand
Cast	Anna Karina, Sady Rebbot, André S. Labarthe, Peter Kassovitz
Format/Duration	B/W, 35mm/85 min.

"Le Nouveau monde" (contribution to *RoGoPaG*)

Production Company	Société Lyre/Arco Film
Direction	Jean-Luc Godard
Screenplay	Jean-Luc Godard
Cinematography	Jean Rabier
Editing	Agnès Guillemot, Lila Lakshmanan
Sound	Hervé
Music	Beethoven
Cast	Alexandra Stewart, Jean-Marc Bory, Jean-André Fieschi, Michel Delahaye
Format/Duration	B/W, 35mm/20 min.

1963

Les Carabiniers / The Soldiers

Production	Georges de Beauregard, Carlo Ponti
Production Company	Rome-Paris Films/Les Films Marceau/Laetitia Films
Direction	Jean-Luc Godard
Screenplay	Jean-Luc Godard, Roberto Rossellini, Jean

	Gruault; from *I Carabinieri* by Benjamino Joppolo
Cinematography	Raoul Coutard
Editing	Agnès Guillemot, Lila Lakshmanan
Sound	Jacques Maumont
Music	Philippe Arthuys
Cast	Marino Masé, Albert Juross, Geneviève Galéa, Catherine Ribeiro
Format/Duration	B/W, 35mm/80 min.

"Le Grand Escroc" (contribution to *Les plus belles escroqueries du monde*

Production	Pierre Roustang
Production Company	Ulysse Productions/Primex Films/Lux/CCF/Vides Cinematografica/Toho/Caesar Productie
Direction	Jean-Luc Godard
Screenplay	Jean-Luc Godard
Cinematography	Raoul Coutard
Editing	Agnès Guillemot, Lila Lakshmanan
Sound	Hervé
Music	Michel Legrand
Cast	Jean Seberg, Charles Denner, Laszlo Szabo
Format/Duration	B/W, 35mm/25 min.

Le Mépris / Contempt

Production	Georges de Beauregard, Carlo Ponti, Joseph E. Levine
Production Company	Rome-Paris Films/Les Films Concordia/Compagnia Cinematografica Champion
Direction	Jean-Luc Godard
Screenplay	Jean-Luc Godard; from *Il Disprezzo* by Alberto Moravia
Cinematography	Raoul Coutard
Editing	Agnès Guillemot, Lila Lakshmanan

Sound	William Sivel
Music	Georges Delerue
Cast	Brigitte Bardot, Michel Piccoli, Jack Palance, Fritz Lang
Format/Duration	Color, 35mm/105 min.

1964

Bande à part / Band of Outsiders

Production Company	Anouchka Films/Orsay Films
Direction	Jean-Luc Godard
Screenplay	Jean-Luc Godard; from *Fool's Gold* by Dolores and Bert Hitchens
Cinematography	Raoul Coutard
Editing	Agnès Guillemot, Françoise Collin
Sound	René Levert, Antoine Bonfanti
Music	Michel Legrand
Cast	Anna Karina, Claude Brasseur, Sami Frey, Louisa Colpeyn
Format/Duration	B/W, 35mm/95 min.

Une Femme mariée / A Married Woman

Production Company	Bnouchka Films/Orsay Films
Direction	Jean-Luc Godard
Screenplay	Jean-Luc Godard
Cinematography	Raoul Coutard
Editing	Agnès Guillemot, Françoise Collin
Sound	René Levert, Antoine Bonfanti
Music	Beethoven, Claude Nougaro
Cast	Macha Méril, Bernard Noël, Philippe Leroy, Roger Leenhardt
Format/Duration	B/W, 35mm/98 min.

1965

Alphaville, une étrange aventure de Lemmy Caution / Alphaville

Production	André Michelin

Production Company	Chaumiane Production/Filmstudio
Direction	Jean-Luc Godard
Screenplay	Jean-Luc Godard
Cinematography	Raoul Coutard
Editing	Agnès Guillemot
Sound	René Levert
Music	Paul Mizraki
Cast	Eddie Constantine, Anna Karina, Akim Tamiroff, Howard Vernon
Format/Duration	B/W, 35mm/98 min.

"Montparnasse-Levallois" (contribution to *Paris vu par . . . / Six in Paris*)

Production	Barbet Schroeder
Production Company	Les Films du Losange
Direction	Jean-Luc Godard
Screenplay	Jean-Luc Godard
Cinematography	Albert Maysles
Editing	Jacqueline Raynal
Sound	René Levert
Cast	Joanna Shimkus, Philippe Hiquily, Serge Davri
Format/Duration	Color, 16mm blown up to 35mm/18 min.

Pierrot le fou

Production	Georges de Beauregard
Production Company	Rome-Paris Films/Dino de Laurentiis Cinematografica
Direction	Jean-Luc Godard
Asst. Directors	Philippe Fourastié, Jean-Pierre Léaud
Screenplay	Jean-Luc Godard; from *Obsession* by Lionel White
Cinematography	Raoul Coutard
Camera Operator	Georges Liron
Editing	Françoise Collin
Art Director	Pierre Guffroy

Sound	René Levert
Music	Antoine Duhamel
Songs	*Jamais je ne t'ai dit que je t'aimerai toujours* and *Ma ligne de chance,* Antoine Duhamel and Bassiak
Format/Duration	Eastman Color, 35mm/110 min.
Shooting	June–July 1965, Paris, South of France
Premiere	Venice Film Festival, 29 August 1965

Cast

Ferdinand	Jean-Paul Belmondo
Marianne	Anna Karina
Fred	Dirk Sanders
Devos	Raymond Devos
Madame Griffon	Graziella Galvani
Gangsters	Roger Dutoit and Hans Meyer
Midget	Jimmy Karoubi
Princess	Princesse Aicha Abidir
Samuel Fuller	Himself
Sailor	Alexis Poliakoff
Dominican Exile	Laszlo Szabo
Cinema spectator	Jean-Pierre Léaud
Others	Pascal Aubier, Pierre Hanin

1966

Masculin Féminin / Masculine Feminine

Production Company	Anouchka Films/Argos Films/Svensk/Filmindustri/Sandrews
Direction	Jean-Luc Godard
Screenplay	Jean-Luc Godard; from "La Femme de Paul" and "Le Signe" by Guy de Maupassant
Cinematography	Willy Kurant
Editing	Agnès Guillemot
Sound	René Levert
Music	Francis Lai, Mozart
Cast	Jean-Pierre Léaud, Chantal Goya, Marlène Jobert, Michel Debord
Format/Duration	B/W, 35mm/110 min.

Made in U.S.A.

Production	Georges de Beauregard
Production Company	Rome-Paris Films/Anouchka Films/SEPIC
Direction	Jean-Luc Godard
Screenplay	Jean-Luc Godard; from *The Jugger* by Richard Stark
Cinematography	Raoul Coutard
Editing	Agnès Guillemot
Sound	René Levert, Jacques Maumont
Music	Beethoven, Schumann, Mick Jagger, Keith Richard
Cast	Anna Karina, Laszlo Szabo, Jean-Pierre Léaud, Yves Alfonso
Format/Duration	Color, 35mm/90 min.

Deux ou trois choses que je sais d'elle / Two or Three Things I Know About Her

Production Company	Anouchka Films/Argos Films/Les Films du Carrosse
Direction	Jean-Luc Godard
Screenplay	Jean-Luc Godard
Cinematography	Raoul Coutard
Editing	Françoise Collin, Chantal Delattre
Sound	René Levert, Antoine Bonfanti
Music	Beethoven
Cast	Marina Vlady, Anny Duperey, Roger Monsoret, Raoul Lévy
Format/Duration	Color, 35mm/90 min.

1967

"Anticipation ou l'amour en l'an 2000" (contribution to *Le Plus vieux métier du monde*)

Production	Joseph Bercholz
Production Company	Francoriz Films/Les Films Gibé/Rialto Films/Rizzoli Films
Direction	Jean-Luc Godard

Screenplay	Jean-Luc Godard
Cinematography	Pierre Lhomme
Editing	Agnès Guillemot
Music	Michel Legrand
Cast	Jacques Charrier, Anna Karina, Marilù Tolo, Jean-Pierre Léaud
Format/Duration	Color, 35mm/20 min.

"Camera-œil" (contribution to *Loin du Viêtnam / Far from Vietnam*)

Production Company	S.L.O.N.
Direction	Jean-Luc Godard
Screenplay	Jean-Luc Godard
Cinematography	Alain Levent
Format/Duration	Color, 16mm/15 min.

La Chinoise, ou plutôt à la chinoise / La Chinoise

Production Company	Anouchka Films/Les Productions de la Guéville/Athos Films/Parc Films/Simar Films
Direction	Jean-Luc Godard
Screenplay	Jean-Luc Godard
Cinematography	Raoul Coutard
Editing	Agnès Guillemot, Delphine Desfons
Sound	René Levert
Music	Stockhausen, Schubert, Vivaldi
Cast	Anne Wiazemsky, Jean-Pierre Léaud, Michel Semeniako, Lex de Bruijn
Format/Duration	Color, 35mm/96 min.

"L'Aller et retour andate e ritorno des enfants prodigues dei figli prodighi" (contribution to *Amore e rabbia/Vangelo 70*)

Production Company	Anouchka Films/Castoro Film
Direction	Jean-Luc Godard
Screenplay	Jean-Luc Godard
Cinematography	Alain Levent
Editing	Agnès Guillemot

Sound	Guy Villette
Music	Giovanni Fusco
Cast	Nino Castelnuovo, Catherine Jourdan, Christine Guého, Paolo Pozzesi
Format/Duration	Color, 35mm/26 min.

Week-end

Production Company	Films Copernic/Ascot Cineraid/Comacico/Lira Films
Direction	Jean-Luc Godard
Screenplay	Jean-Luc Godard
Cinematography	Raoul Coutard
Editing	Agnès Guillemot
Sound	René Levert
Music	Antoine Duhamel, Mozart, Guy Béart
Cast	Mireille Darc, Jean Yanne, Jean-Pierre Kalfon, Jean-Pierre Léaud
Format/Duration	Color, 35mm/95 min.

1968

Le Gai savoir

Production Company	Anouchka Films/Bavaria Atelier/O.R.T.F./Suddeutschen Rundfunk
Direction	Jean-Luc Godard
Screenplay	Jean-Luc Godard
Cinematography	Georges Leclerc
Editing	Germaine Cohen
Music	Cuban Revolutionary Songs
Cast	Jean-Pierre Léaud, Juliet Berto
Format/Duration	Color, 35mm/95 min.

Ciné-tracts (series of 2- to 4-minute shorts)

Production	Jean-Luc Godard, others
Format	B/W, 16mm.

Un Film comme les autres / A Film Like Any Other

Production	Groupe Dziga Vertov
Production Company	Anouchka Films
Format/Duration	Color, 16mm/100 min.

One Plus One (Sympathy for the Devil)

Production	Iain Quarrier, Michael Pearson
Production Company	Cupid Productions Inc.
Direction	Jean-Luc Godard
Screenplay	Jean-Luc Godard
Cinematography	Anthony Richmond
Editing	Ken Rowles
Sound	Arthur Bradburn
Music	The Rolling Stones
Cast	Anne Wiazemsky, Iain Quarrier, Danny Daniels, The Rolling Stones
Format/Duration	Color, 35mm/99 min.

One American Movie (One A.M.) (abandoned during production, footage incorporated in One P.M. [One Parallel Movie], released in 1971)

Production Company	Leacock/Pennebaker Inc.
Direction	Jean-Luc Godard, D.A. Pennebaker
Screenplay	Jean-Luc Godard, D.A. Pennebaker
Cinematography	Richard Leacock, D.A. Pennebaker
Editing	Richard Leacock, D.A. Pennebaker
Cast	Richard Leacock, D.A. Pennebaker, Jean-Luc Godard, Eldridge Cleaver
Format/Duration	Color, 16mm/90 min.

1969

British Sounds (See You at Mao)

Production Company	Kestrel Productions, for London Weekend Television
Direction	Jean-Luc Godard, Jean-Henri Roger

Screenplay	Jean-Luc Godard, Jean-Henri Roger
Cinematography	Charles Stewart
Editing	Elizabeth Koziman
Sound	Fred Sharp
Format/Duration	Color, 16mm/52 min.

Pravda

Production	Claude Nedjar
Production Company	Centre Européen Cinéma Radio Télévision
Direction	Groupe Dziga Vertov
Screenplay	Groupe Dziga Vertov
Cinematography	Groupe Dziga Vertov
Editing	Groupe Dziga Vertov
Sound	Groupe Dziga Vertov
Format/Duration	Color, 16mm/58 min.

Vent d'est / Wind from the East

Production Company	Poli Film/Anouchka Films/Kuntz Film
Direction	Groupe Dziga Vertov
Screenplay	Jean-Luc Godard, Daniel Cohn-Bendit, Sergio Bazzini
Cinematography	Mario Vulpiani
Editing	Jean-Luc Godard, Jean-Pierre Gorin
Sound	Antonio Ventura, Carlo Diotalleri
Cast	Gian Maria Volonté, Anne Wiazemsky, Paolo Pozzesi, Christiana Tullio Altan
Format/Duration	Color, 16mm/100 min.

Luttes en Italie (Lotte in Italia)

Production Company	Cosmoseion for RAI
Direction	Groupe Dziga Vertov
Screenplay	Groupe Dziga Vertov
Cast	Anne Wiazemsky, Paolo Pozzesi, Christiana Tullio Altan, Jérôme Hinstin
Format/Duration	Color, 16mm/76 min.

1970

Jusqu'à la victoire (incomplete; footage incorporated in *Ici et ailleurs*)

Production Company	Groupe Dziga Vertov
Direction	Groupe Dziga Vertov

1971

Vladimir et Rosa / Vladimir and Rosa

Production Company	Grove Press Evergreen Films/Telepool
Direction	Groupe Dziga Vertov
Screenplay	Groupe Dziga Vertov
Cinematography	Groupe Dziga Vertov
Cast	Anne Wiazemsky, Jean-Pierre Gorin, Juliet Berto, Ernest Menzer
Format/Duration	Color, 16mm/106 min.

1972

Tout va bien

Production	Alain Coiffier, Jean-Pierre Rassam, Jean-Luc Godard
Production Company	Anouchka Films/Vicco Films/Empire Film
Direction	Jean-Luc Godard, Jean-Pierre Gorin
Screenplay	Jean-Luc Godard, Jean-Pierre Gorin
Cinematography	Armand Marco
Editing	Kenout Peltier
Sound	Bernard Ortion, Armand Bonfanti
Music	Eric Charden, Thomas Rivat, Paul Beuscher
Cast	Yves Montand, Jane Fonda, Vittorio Caprioli, Jean Pignol
Format/Duration	Color, 35mm/95 min.

Letter to Jane

Production Company	Jean-Luc Godard, Jean-Pierre Gorin
Direction	Jean-Luc Godard, Jean-Pierre Gorin

Screenplay	Jean-Luc Godard, Jean-Pierre Gorin
Format/Duration	Color, 16mm/52 min.

1974

Ici et ailleurs / Here and Elsewhere

Production Company	Sonimage/I.N.A.
Direction	Jean-Luc Godard, Anne-Marie Miéville
Screenplay	Jean-Luc Godard, Anne-Marie Miéville
Cinematography	William Lubtchansky
Editing	Anne-Marie Miéville (footage from *Jusqu'à la victoire*)
Format/Duration	Color, 16mm/55 min.

1975

Numéro deux

Production Company	Sonimage/Bela Prod./S.N.C.
Direction	Jean-Luc Godard
Screenplay	Jean-Luc Godard, Anne-Marie Miéville
Cinematography	William Lubtchansky
Video	Gérard Teissèdre
Sound	Jean-Pierre Ruh
Music	Léo Ferré
Cast	Sandrine Battistella, Pierre Oudry, Alexandre Rignault, Rachel Stefanopoli
Format/Duration	Color, 35mm, video/88 min.

1976

Comment ça va

Production Company	Sonimage/I.N.A./Bela Prod./S.N.C.
Direction	Jean-Luc Godard, Anne-Marie Miéville
Screenplay	Jean-Luc Godard, Anne-Marie Miéville
Cinematography	William Lubtchansky
Music	Jean Schwartz
Cast	Anne-Marie Miéville, M. Marot
Format/Duration	Color, 16mm/78 min.

Six fois deux/Sur et sous la communication (Ya personne/
Louison; Leçons de choses/Jean-Luc; Photo et cie/Marcel; Pas
d'histoires/Nanas; Nous trois/René(e)s; Avant et
après/Jacqueline et Ludovic)

Production Company	Sonimage/I.N.A.
Direction	Jean-Luc Godard, Anne-Marie Miéville
Screenplay	Jean-Luc Godard, Anne-Marie Miéville
Cinematography	William Lubtchansky, Gérard Teissèdre
Editing	Jean-Luc Godard, Anne-Marie Miéville
Format/Duration	Color, video/6 × 100 min.

1977–8

France/tour/détour/deux enfants (Obscur/Chimie; Lumière/
Physique; Connu/Géométrie/Géographie; Inconnu/Technique;
Impression/Dictée; Expression/Français; Violence/Grammaire;
Désordre/Calcul; Pouvoir/Musique; Roman/Économie; Réalité/
Logique; Rêve/Morale)

Production Company	I.N.A. for Antenne 2/Sonimage
Direction	Jean-Luc Godard, Jean-Pierre Melville
Screenplay	Jean-Luc Godard, Jean-Pierre Melville
Cinematography	Pierre Binggeli, William Lubtchansky, Dominique Chapuis, Philippe Rony
Cast	Camille Virolleaud, Arnaud Martin, Betty Berr, Albert Dray
Format/Duration	Color, video/12 × 26 min.

1979

Scénario de Sauve qui peut (la vie)

Production Company	JLG Films
Direction	Jean-Luc Godard
Format/Duration	Color, video/20 min.

Sauve qui peut (la vie) / *Every Man for Himself*

Production	Alain Sarde, Jean-Luc Godard
Production Company	Sara Films/MK2/Saga Production/Sonimage/C.N.C./Z.D.F./S.S.R./O.R.F.

Direction	Jean-Luc Godard
Screenplay	Anne-Marie Miéville, Jean-Claude Carrière
Cinematography	William Lubtchansky, Renato Berta, Jean-Bernard Menoud
Editing	Jean-Luc Godard, Anne-Marie Miéville
Sound	Jacques Maumont, Luc Yersin, Oscar Stellavox
Music	Gabriel Yared
Cast	Isabelle Huppert, Jacques Dutronc, Nathalie Baye, Cécile Tanner, Roland Amstutz
Format/Duration	Color, 35mm/87 min.

1981

Lettre à Freddy Buache

Production Company	Film et Vidéo Productions
Direction	Jean-Luc Godard, Pierre Binggeli, Gérard Rucy
Screenplay	Jean-Luc Godard
Cinematography	Jean-Bernard Menoud
Editing	Jean-Luc Godard
Sound	François Musy
Music	Ravel
Format/Duration	Video transferred to 35mm color/11 min.

1982

"Changer d'image" (contribution to broadcast *Le Changement a plus d'un titre*)

Direction	Jean-Luc Godard
Cast	Jean-Luc Godard
Format/Duration	Color, video/9 min.

Passion

Production	Alain Sarde
Production Company	Sara Films/Sonimage/Films A2/Film et Vidéo Production/S.S.R.
Direction	Jean-Luc Godard

Screenplay	Jean-Luc Godard
Cinematography	Raoul Coutard
Editing	Jean-Luc Godard
Sound	François Musy
Music	Mozart, Dvořák, Ravel, Beethoven, Fauré
Cast	Isabelle Huppert, Hanna Schygulla, Michel Piccoli, Jerzy Radziwilowicz, Laszlo Szabo
Format/Duration	Color, 35mm/87 min.

Scénario du film Passion

Production Company	JLG Films/Studio TransVidéo/Télévision Suisse Romande
Direction	Jean-Luc Godard, Jean-Bernard Menoud, Anne-Marie Miéville, Pierre Binggeli
Format/Duration	Color, video/54 min.

1983

Prénom Carmen / First Name Carmen

Production	Alain Sarde
Production Company	Sara Films/JLG Films
Direction	Jean-Luc Godard
Screenplay	Anne-Marie Miéville
Cinematography	Raoul Coutard, Jean Garcenot
Editing	Suzanne Lang-Villar, Jean-Luc Godard
Sound	François Musy
Music	Beethoven, Tom Waits
Cast	Maruschka Detmers, Jacques Bonnafé, Myriem Roussel, Christophe Odent
Format/Duration	Color, 35mm/85 min.

Petites notes à propos du film Je vous salue Marie

Production Company	JLG Films
Direction	Jean-Luc Godard
Cast	Jean-Luc Godard, Myriem Roussel, Thierry Rode, Anne-Marie Miéville
Format/Duration	Color, video/25 min.

1985

Je vous salue Marie / Hail Mary (intended for screening with Anne-Marie Miéville's *Le Livre de Marie)*

Production Company	Pégase Films/S.S.R./JLG Films/Sara Films/Channel 4
Direction	Jean-Luc Godard
Screenplay	Jean-Luc Godard
Cinematography	Jean-Bernard Menoud, Jacques Firmann
Editing	Anne-Marie Miéville
Sound	François Musy
Music	Bach, Dvořák, Coltrane
Cast	Myriem Roussel, Thierry Rode, Philippe Lacoste, Anne Gauthier, Juliette Binoche
Format/Duration	Color, 35mm/72 min.

Détective

Production Company	Sara Films/JLG Films
Direction	Jean-Luc Godard
Screenplay	Alain Sarde, Philippe Setbon, Anne-Marie Miéville
Cinematography	Bruno Nuytten
Editing	Marilyne Dubreuil
Sound	Pierre Gamet, François Musy
Music	Schubert, Wagner, Chopin, Liszt, Honegger, Chabrier, Ornette Coleman, Jean Schwarz
Cast	Nathalie Baye, Claude Brasseur, Johnny Hallyday, Jean-Pierre Léaud
Format/Duration	Color, 35mm/95 min.

1986

Grandeur et décadence d'un petit commerce de cinéma

Production	Pierre Grimblat
Production Company	TF1/"Série Noire"/Hamster Prod./JLG Films
Direction	Jean-Luc Godard
Screenplay	Jean-Luc Godard
Cinematography	Caroline Champetier, Serge Le François

Sound	François Musy, Pierre-Alain Besse
Music	Bartók, Leonard Cohen, Bob Dylan, Janis Joplin, Joni Mitchell
Cast	Jean-Pierre Léaud, Jean-Pierre Mocky, Marie Valera
Format/Duration	Color, 16mm/52 min.

Soft and Hard (A Soft Conversation Between Two Friends on a Hard Subject)

Production Company	JLG Films/Channel 4
Direction	Jean-Luc Godard, Anne-Marie Miéville
Cast	Jean-Luc Godard. Anne-Marie Miéville
Format/Duration	Color, video/48 min.

J.L.G. Meets W.A./Meetin' WA

Production Company	Jean-Luc Godard
Direction	Jean-Luc Godard
Cast	Woody Allen, Jean-Luc Godard
Format/Duration	Color, video/26 min.

1987

"Armide" (contribution to *Aria*)

Production	Don Boyd
Production Company	Lightyear Entertainment/Virgin Vision
Direction	Jean-Luc Godard
Cinematography	Caroline Champetier
Editing	Jean-Luc Godard
Music	Lully
Cast	Marion Peterson, Valérie Allain, Jacques Neuville, Luke Corre
Format/Duration	Color, 35mm/12 min.

King Lear

Production	Menahem Golan, Yoram Globus
Production Company	Cannon Films
Direction	Jean-Luc Godard

Screenplay	Jean-Luc Godard; from *King Lear* by William Shakespeare
Cinematography	Sophie Maintigneux
Editing	Jean-Luc Godard
Sound	François Musy
Cast	Burgess Meredith, Peter Sellars, Molly Ringwald, Norman Mailer, Jean-Luc Godard
Format/Duration	Color, 35mm/90 min.

Soigne ta droite / Keep Up Your Right

Production	Philippe DeChaise Martin
Production Company	Gaumont/JLG Films/Xanadu Films
Direction	Jean-Luc Godard
Screenplay	Jean-Luc Godard
Cinematography	Caroline Champetier
Editing	Jean-Luc Godard
Sound	François Musy
Music	Rita Mitsouko
Cast	Jean-Luc Godard, Jacques Villeret, François Périer, Jane Birkin
Format/Duration	Color, 35mm/82 min.

1988

On s'est tous défilé

Production Company	JLG Films
Direction	Jean-Luc Godard
Format/Duration	Color, video/13 min.

Puissance de la parole

Production Company	Gaumont/JLG Films/France Télécom
Direction	Jean-Luc Godard
Cinematography	Caroline Champetier, Pierre-Alain Besse
Sound	François Musy, Pierre-Alain Besse, Marc-Antoine Beldent
Music	Bach, Beethoven, Cage, Richard Strauss, Franck, Ravel, Leonard Cohen, Bob Dylan

Cast	Jean Bouise, Laurence Cote, Lydia Andrei, Michel Iribarren
Format/Duration	Color, video/25 min.

"Le Dernier mot" / "Les Français entendus par" (contribution to broadcast *Les Français vus par)*

Production	Anne-Marie Miéville, Hervé Duhamel, Marie-Christine Barrière
Production Company	Erato Films/Socpresse/Le Figaro/JLG Films
Direction	Jean-Luc Godard
Cinematography	Pierre Binggeli
Sound	Pierre Camus, Raoul Fruhauf, François Musy
Music	Bach
Cast	André Marcon, Hans Zichter, Catherine Aymerie, Pierre Amoyal
Format/Duration	Color, video/13 min.

1989

Le Rapport Darty

Direction	Jean-Luc Godard, Anne-Marie Miéville
Cast	Jean-Luc Godard, Anne-Marie Miéville
Format/Duration	Color, video/50 min.

1990

Nouvelle vague / New Wave

Production	Alain Sarde, Ruth Waldburger
Production Company	Sara Films/Périphéria/Canal +/Véga Films/Télévision Suisse Romande/Films A2/C.N.C./Sofia Investimage/Sofia Créations
Direction	Jean-Luc Godard
Screenplay	Jean-Luc Godard
Cinematography	William Lubtchansky
Editing	Jean-Luc Godard
Sound	François Musy
Cast	Alain Delon, Domiziana Giordano, Roland Amstutz, Laurence Cote

Format/Duration   Color, 35mm/89 min.

"L'Enfance de l'art" (contribution to *Comment vont les enfants /
How Are the Kids*)

Production Company JLG Films/UNICEF
Direction   Jean-Luc Godard, Anne-Marie Miéville
Screenplay   Jean-Luc Godard, Anne-Marie Miéville
Format/Duration   Color, 35mm/8 min.

1991

Allemagne année 90 neuf zéro / Germany Year 90 Nine Zero

Production   Nicole Ruelle
Production Company Antenne 2/Brainstorm Productions
Direction   Jean-Luc Godard
Screenplay   Jean-Luc Godard; from *Nos Solitudes* by
                         Michel Hanoun
Cinematography   Christophe Pollock, Andréas Erben, Stépan
                         Benda
Sound   Pierre-Alain Besse, François Musy
Music   Bryars, Scelsi, Liszt, Mozart, Bach,
                         Stravinsky, Hindemith, Beethoven,
                         Shostakovitch
Cast   Eddie Constantine, Hanns Zischler, Claudia
                         Michelsen, André S. Labarthe, Nathalie Kadem
Format/Duration   Color, 35mm/62 min.

1992

Contribution to *Contre l'oubli / Lest We Forget*

Production Company Les Films du Paradoxe/PRV/Amnesty
                         International
Format/Duration   Color, 35mm/110 min.

1993

Hélas pour moi / Woe Is Me

Production   Ruth Waldburger

Production Company	Les Films Alain Sarde/Véga Films
Direction	Jean-Luc Godard
Screenplay	Jean-Luc Godard; from *Amphitryon 38* by Jean Giraudoux
Cinematography	Caroline Champetier
Sound	François Musy
Music	Bach, Shostakovitch, Beethoven, Tchaikovsky, Honegger
Cast	Gérard Depardieu, Laurence Masliah, Bernard Verley, Jean-Louis Loca
Format/Duration	Color, 35mm/85 min.

1994

JLG/JLG (Autoportrait de décembre) / JLG/JLG (Self-Portrait in December)

Production	Jean-Luc Godard
Production Company	Gaumont/Périphéria
Direction	Jean-Luc Godard
Screenplay	Jean-Luc Godard
Cinematography	Yves Pouliquen, Christian Jaquenod
Editing	Catherine Cormon
Cast	Jean-Luc Godard, Denis Jadot
Format/Duration	Color, 35mm/63 min.

Les Enfants jouent à la Russie / The Children Play Russian

Production	Ruth Waldburger
Production Company	JLG Films
Direction	Jean-Luc Godard
Screenplay	Jean-Luc Godard
Cinematography	Christophe Pollock
Editing	Jean-Luc Godard
Cast	Laszlo Szabo, Bernard Eisenschitz, Jean-Luc Godard, André S. Labarthe
Format/Duration	Color, video/63 min.

1995

2 × 50 ans de cinéma français / 2 × 50 Years of French Cinema

Production	Colin MacCabe, Bob Last
Production Company	Périphéria/BFI TV/La Sept/ARTE
Direction	Anne-Marie Miéville, Jean-Luc Godard
Screenplay	Anne-Marie Miéville, Jean-Luc Godard
Cinematography	Anne-Marie Miéville, Jean-Luc Godard
Format/Duration	Color, video/51 min.

1996

Forever Mozart / For Ever Mozart

Production	Ruth Waldburger, Alain Sarde
Production Company	Véga Films/Avventura Films/Périphéria/ECM
Direction	Jean-Luc Godard
Screenplay	Jean-Luc Godard
Cinematography	Christophe Pollock
Editing	Jean-Luc Godard
Sound	François Musy, Olivier Burgaud
Music	David Darling, Ketil Bjornstad, Ben Harper, Györgi Kurtag
Cast	Madeleine Assas, Ghalia Lacroix, Bérangère Allaux, Vicky Messica, Frédéric Pierrot
Format/Duration	Color, 35mm/85 min.

1989-96

Histoire(s) du cinéma (ongoing project; eight parts completed as of 1996 Part 1A – Toutes les histoires; 1B – Une Histoire seule [1989]; 2A – Seul le cinéma; 2B – Fatale beauté [1994]; 3A – La Monnaie de l'absolu/La Réponse des ténèbres; 3B – Montage, mon beau souci/Une Vague nouvelle; 4A – Le Contrôle de l'univers; 4B – Les Signes parmi nous [1996])

Production Company	Gaumont/JLG Films/La Sept/Fr 3/Centre National de la Cinématographie/Radio Télévision Suisse Romande/Véga Films

Direction	Jean-Luc Godard
Screenplay	Jean-Luc Godard
Editing	Jean-Luc Godard
Format/Duration	Color, video/Part 1a, 1b, 50 min.; 2a, 2b, 25 min.; 3a, 3b, 4a, 4b, 25 min.

Additional Films Cited

Barbarella, dir. Roger Vadim (France/Italy, 1967)
Bonjour Tristesse, dir. Otto Preminger (Columbia, USA, 1958)
Bonnie and Clyde, dir. Arthur Penn (Warner Bros., USA, 1967)
Borsalino, dir. Jacques Deray (France, 1969)
Borsalino et Co.(Blood on the Streets), dir. Jacques Deray (France, 1974)
Les Bronzés, dir. Patrice Leconte (France, 1978)
Buffet froid, dir. Bertrand Blier (France, 1979)
Casablanca, dir. Michael Curtiz (Warner Bros., USA, 1942)
Le Cercle rouge (The Red Circle), dir. Jean-Pierre Melville (France/Italy, 1970)
Le Chagrin et la pitié (The Sorrow and the Pity), dir. Marcel Ophuls (France, 1970)
China Gate, dir. Samuel Fuller (Twentieth Century Fox, USA, 1957)
Coup de torchon (Clean Slate), dir. Bertrand Tavernier (France, 1981)
Design for Living, dir. Ernst Lubitsch (Paramount, USA, 1933)
Dial M for Murder, dir. Alfred Hitchcock (Warner Bros., USA, 1954)
La Femme infidèle (The Unfaithful Wife), dir. Claude Chabrol (France/Italy, 1969)
Forty Guns, dir. Samuel Fuller (Twentieth Century Fox, USA, 1957)
The French Connection, dir. William Friedkin (Twentieth Century Fox, USA, 1971)
High Sierra, dir. Raoul Walsh (Warner Bros., USA, 1941)
House of Bamboo, dir. Samuel Fuller (Twentieth Century Fox, USA, 1955)
India Song, dir. Marguerite Duras (France, 1975)
Lacombe Lucien, dir. Louis Malle (France/Italy/West Germany, 1974)
Lola Montès, dir. Max Ophuls (France, 1955)
Les Maîtres fous, dir. Jean Rouch (France, 1955)
Mauvais sang (Bad Blood), dir. Léos Carax (France, 1986)
Les Mistons (The Mischief Makers), dir. François Truffaut (France, 1957)
The Most Dangerous Game, dir. Irving Pichel and Ernst Schoedsack (RKO, USA, 1932)

Nada (The Nada Gang), dir. Claude Chabrol (France, 1974)

Napoléon vu par Abel Gance (Napoleon), dir. Abel Gance (France, 1927)

Natural Born Killers, dir. Oliver Stone (Universal, USA, 1994)

Son Nom de Venise dans Calcutta désert, dir. Marguerite Duras (France, 1976)

La Nuit américaine (Day for Night), dir. François Truffaut (France/Italy, 1973)

Orphée (Orpheus), dir. Jean Cocteau (France, 1950)

La Passion Béatrice (Beatrice), dir. Bertrand Tavernier (France, 1987)

La Passion de Jeanne d'Arc (The Passion of Joan of Arc), dir. Carl Dreyer (France, 1928)

Le Père Noël est une ordure (Santa Claus Is a Louse), dir. Jean-Marie Poiré (France, 1982)

Mes Petites amoureuses (My Little Loves), dir. Jean Eustache (France, 1974)

Pickpocket, dir. Robert Bresson (France, 1959)

Pickup on South Street, dir. Samuel Fuller (Twentieth Century Fox, USA, 1953)

Psycho, dir. Alfred Hitchcock (Universal, USA, 1960)

Pulp Fiction, dir. Quentin Tarantino (Miramax, USA, 1994)

14 juillet (July 14th), dir. René Clair (France, 1933)

La Règle du jeu (The Rules of the Game), dir. Jean Renoir (France, 1939)

Reservoir Dogs, dir. Quentin Tarantino (Miramax, USA, 1992)

Sac de nœuds, dir. Bertrand Blier (France, 1985)

Le Samouraï (The Samurai), dir. Jean-Pierre Melville (France/Italy, 1967)

Shock Corridor, dir. Samuel Fuller (Columbia, USA, 1963)

Souvenirs d'en France (French Provincial), dir. André Téchiné (France, 1975)

Tenue de soirée (Ménage), dir. Bertrand Blier (France, 1986)

Tirez sur le pianiste (Shoot the Piano Player), dir. François Truffaut (France, 1960)

Topaz, dir. Alfred Hitchcock (Universal, USA, 1969)

Touchez pas au grisbi (Grisbi), dir. Jacques Becker (France/Italy, 1954)

Traité de bave et d'éternité, dir. Isidore Isou (France, 1951)

Trop belle pour toi (Too Beautiful for You), dir. Bertrand Blier (France, 1989)

Les Valseuses (Going Places), dir. Bertrand Blier (France, 1973)

La Vie de famille, dir. Jacques Doillon (France, 1985)

Reviews of *Pierrot le fou*

"PIERROT LE FOU"

JEAN DE BARONCELLI

Le Monde, 9 November 1965, reprinted with permission.

Either one considers the cinema to be an industry whose products should respond exactly to public demand, or one admits that it can "also" be an art, as André Malraux declared the other day from the tribune of the Chambre des députés, humorously reversing the terms of a formula that he has made famous.

In the first case it is doubtless natural to be scandalized by Jean-Luc Godard's movies and to see nothing in this author but a "fraud," a "little clown," who is having one over on us. This is a classic reaction. In art as in politics, the public is instinctively conservative. It only likes what it knows. Faced with novelty, it smells danger. It sneers, it hurls insults, or, like a snail, it retreats into its shell.

Pierrot le fou risks causing many spectators to retreat into their shells. They simply do not have the same conception of cinema as Jean-Luc Godard. Godard's is resolutely optimistic. And passionate. It is not enough to say that Godard loves the cinema. He adores it. It is under his skin. He believes in its past, its present, and its future. In its future above all, since one cannot imagine an art that is not continually evolving.

So, as others are with literature, music, or painting, Godard is at odds with the cinema. He shakes it, shoves it, maltreats it; he strives to pull it out of the ruts that laziness has gotten it into, he

tries to push it forward along new paths; in short, he accomplishes
in his own way his duties as a creator.

Such are the vicissitudes of this loving struggle that is presented
to us in the form of films. One could obviously judge this sort of
attempt as vain, puerile or superfluous. But before denigrating it
let us at least try to understand it. In contrast to the cinema that,
since the arrival of the talkies (things were different in the silent
age) seems to have assigned itself the essential role of carefully
telling stories in images, Godard prefers a cinema "charged" with
emotion – like a bullet is "charged" with powder – the emotion
inspired by the film being, in the end, only the reflection of that
felt by the director. In other words, Godard wants cinema to take
the step that was taken by painting a long time ago. This is why,
from film to film, he behaves more and more aggressively toward
the arsenal of conventions, rules, and routines that weigh down
and paralyze cinematic expression. To break through the bars, to
tear down the barricades, to give back to cinema its primitive liberty (that of silent film) in order to assure the complete freedom of
the author: such is his intent. However, this freedom is not to be
confused with anarchy, and the author only uses it to reveal to us
what is most intimate to himself, his secrets and dreams.

At the beginning of *Pierrot le fou* there is an adventure novel,
one of those stories full of incidents, accidents and developments
whose rigorous sequence of events is designed to captivate the
public, that is to say to make it believe in the reality of what it is
being told. But that is not the reality that interests Godard. What
interests him is the interior reality, the poetic reality if you will, of
this love-crazy boy, crazy for the absolute, crazy about liberty,
seized by the folly of believing that one can escape the idiocy of
our civilization, that one can flee with impunity into the sun with
the woman one loves, that one can love without mistrust, enjoy
the trees and the ocean; in short, that he can be happy with no
more than a deserted island, when betrayal, ugliness, violence and
death are everywhere.

From this arises such a syncopated story where the elements of
the original anecdote are only indicated through references; from
this arise the escapades, the songs, the dances, this marveling
before the marvels of nature; from this arise the monologues, the
readings, the jokes, the about-faces, the capers, all of these more

or less comprehensible things which seem to be outside the action but which in truth bring us back to it, which *are* the action.

From this arises also the eminently personal character of the story. By reason of his conception of cinema, Godard has always only told of himself in his films. He has only ever made films in the first person. Whether he is speaking to us of war, love, jealousy, of married women, arms trafficking, or life written in stellar capitals, he always places himself first and foremost on the screen, with his tastes, his manias, his obsessions, his admirations, his dreams. His films, and *Pierrot le fou* possibly more than any other, are the result of interior forces, of subjective currents, of emotions of which he himself seems unconscious. Along with Picasso, whom he loves so much, he could say "It comes to me from far away"; or, like Stendhal on love, he could speak of "crystallization."

This is no doubt why one can only pass an intuitive judgment on a film of this genre. One either likes it or one does not. Instinctively, immediately. If one grows tense, if one fights, if one refuses a minimum of sympathy with the author, if one does not feel complicity, all is lost. And one will not even be grateful to Godard for trying to renovate and refresh our impoverished cinematic language.

In closing, I would like to offer a quote from Whistler in his polemic with Ruskin that seems very applicable to *Pierrot le fou*. Speaking of academic painters, Whistler said: "their works may be finished, but they have not yet begun." One could say the same for hundreds of films. *Pierrot le fou*, on the other hand, may not be a "finished" film, but it has quite certainly "begun."

(Translated by David Laatsch and David Wills)

"PIERROT LE FOU"

MICHAEL KLEIN

Film Quarterly 19, 3 (1966): 46–48, © 1966 by The Regents of the University of California. Reprinted with permission.

Pierrot le Fou opens at night with scenes of a river while a voice (Belmondo) reads to us about Velázquez the painter, we are told, of twilight, silence, and space at the time of the *auto da fe*.

This is a transformation of the opening of *Le Petit Soldat* – Bruno driving into Switzerland at twilight telling us not about Velázquez but Klee. The opening scene of *Pierrot le Fou* comments on a bourgeois party that occurs a bit later. Inside the room there is loud talk and no space; instead of the modulated shadows of Velázquez we see color and at times everything is red. There is no Inquisition, but the quality of life is tense and sterile. People pledge loyalty in an automatic way to the new gods; they speak pop talk; the men plug the virtues of Oldsmobile; the women touch their hair and advertise their brand of hairspray.

Then we see Belmondo at the party. He faces us with his back to a bar. There is a girl on his right. To his left there is a man in dark glasses. The man tells us he is Sam Fuller, an American filmmaker, and defines film as a "battleground: love, hate, action, violence, death; in a word, emotion." Because Belmondo cannot understand American, the girl translates Fuller's statement into French. This scene derives from *Le Mépris*. It is taken in a single long shot and is not intense but distanced from us. Fuller, unlike Palance, is not developed into an epic figure and disappears from the film. His values, however, which are an extension of the romanticism of *Le Mépris,* are acted out in *Pierrot le Fou* as dull and inane.

After Belmondo leaves the party (his wife remains behind flirting with an important business contact) he drives away on an anarchic fling with Karina, his babysitter. They stop at a gas station to refuel, and after a Zazie-like slapstick fight with the attendants, drive away without paying. It resembles the red gas station that Bardot and Palance stop at near the end of *Le Mépris*. It is a "Total Gas" station – at this moment total freedom and total chance seem to be the laws of *Pierrot le Fou*. Soon, however, they have to abandon their red Peugeot because the cops are after them. They calmly drive it next to a wreck whose occupants look like cardboard victims in a Drive Safely display. Karina shoots the gas tank, and the Peugeot goes up in flames. Then they walk away from us into a large green field – this is shown in a long shot that is held until they are far off.

Soon they steal a Ford (again cool slapstick mostly shown from a distance in a static long shot) and have a conversation about freedom. Belmondo demonstrates that he is not bound to travel straight down the road by making a sharp right turn and driving into the calm ocean. Again this is shown to us in a static long shot, and the characters seem small and insignificant in relation to the natural setting.

A sense of insignificance pervades *Pierrot le Fou*, quite unlike the romantic nihilism so frequent in Godard. In this respect *Pierrot le Fou* is unlike *Le Mépris* where, working with Homeric parallels, Godard elevated Bardot and Palance to the status of epic people who could not live in the real world. In *Le Mépris* the recurrent music and the first image (the camera slowly approaching us) expressed a determinism both psychological and external that infused the film, and gave the final sequence at the temple-like stairs an aura of magnificence and loss. In *Pierrot le Fou* the determinism remains. Although Belmondo makes flamboyant attempts to change his life the film ends with Belmondo a suicide and Karina shot by accident. It is summed up in a story Karina tells early in the film about a man who flees Paris to avoid death but is killed in a car crash en route to the Riviera. However the determinism is not expressed in the rhythm of *Pierrot le Fou*, which is very slack. This is a sign of Godard's new style.

The middle of the film, as in *Le Mépris*, is a long domestic scene. Belmondo and Karina attempt to find freedom and happiness in a very stylized and prolonged idyll in nature. Belmondo sits near the ocean with a parrot, putting down his few experiences in a notebook in late Joyce style. Karina wanders very bored along the shore casting rocks into the ocean, repeating and repeating that she wants to have some fun. The problem is that they are not able to enjoy any of the emotions that Fuller speaks of at the start of the film. Karina complains to Belmondo "You speak to me with words, and I look at you with emotions." But neither words nor emotions have any intensity. Stealing and wrecking cars, going on the road without any money or responsibility, an interlude of contemplation and study at the beach – all are dull. Belmondo manages to drift through the idyll but Karina, like the girl in *Une Femme Mariée*, is just bored.

Karina also seems bored with making the film. In one scene she stabs a dwarf who is walking round her brandishing a pistol looking a lot like the Bruno-Godard young man with a camera who photographed Karina in *Le Petit Soldat*. In that film Karina was a "little girl from a play by Giraudoux" and carried a toy dog;

now she is old, bored and the toy animal has become a combination toy and purse, Godard's use of personal experience is in tension with a more objective quality, a strained intellectualization that makes the film at once a bit slack and tumescent. There is a certain incongruity in the style, as there is in Poe whose *William Wilson* is alluded to in the film, something like the expansive dullness of Welles's Kafka; Godard seems to be working to express a new content. Public as well as private events are seen from this point of view. The war in Vietnam is shown in a cross between a comic strip (the character's clothes change) and the style of a Chinese political play. Belmondo is dressed as an American sailor; he brandishes a gun at Karina who is in yellow-face and begs for her life in pidgin-Vietnamese. Several American tourists watch ("I like that, I like that a lot," they say). At the end of the film Belmondo paints his face blue, and runs along a cliff flapping two batches of dynamite, trying to fly. He wraps the dynamite around his head, like a fence, and lights the fuse. From a distance of about a hundred yards we are shown the explosion. Belmondo's final withdrawal is as absurd as the war and the popgun battles the film has shown us. The immolation refers back both to Vietnam and to the *auto da fe,* to a history of futile destruction and self-destruction. (Pierrot's real name is Ferdinand. Godard makes this stick in our mind by often having Karina call him Pierrot to which he always retorts: "My name is Ferdinand." Ferdinand was the name of the king of Spain during the *auto da fe;* it is also the name of the prince who inspires Miranda to think of the "brave new world" that in this century has become a metaphor for the wasteland.)

The coolness that pervades the film, as I have said, is best expressed in Godard's use of long shots, by which I mean that the actors are photographed from a distance for a duration of time, that there is little dynamic action within the frame, that the camera does not move. The shot of Belmondo and Karina disappearing into the lush green landscape is quite unlike, for example, the shot from a distance of Palance striding back and forth on a stage-like embankment in *Le Mépris.* This coolness extends to the way figures and blocs of color are composed – the tense and taut beauty of composition in the long shots of *Le Mépris,* perhaps derived from the architecture of the gun battle near the end of

Lang's *Rancho Notorious,* is rarely found in *Pierrot le Fou.* The key to the style of *Pierrot le Fou,* then, seems to me to be Godard's use of the long shot. Here let me refer to Eisenstein.

> And doesn't what is said here about written language seem a duplication of the clumsy long shot, which, when it attempts to present something dramatically, hopelessly looks like a florid awkward phrase, full of subordinate clauses, participles and adverbs of a "theatrical" *mise-en-scène* with which it dooms itself? . . . One may speak of the *phrase* as the author of "A Discussion of Old and New Style in the Russian Language," the Slavophile Alexander Shishikov, wrote of words: "In language both long and short words are necessary; for without short ones language would sound like the long-drawn-out moo of the cow, and without long ones like the short monotonous chirp of the magpie." (*Film Form,* pp. 249–250)

What is happening is that Godard has taken the equivalent in film language to the long, complex, hypotactically structured sentence of old-style novels and used it to tell a tale that, regarded as a sequence of actions, is dramatic and paratactic. The result is a pop incongruity that, if we are overcome, renders absurd both the old style of telling and our dreams of a new style of living.

"PIERROT LE FOU"

TOM MILNE

Sight and Sound 34, 1 (1965–66): 6–7, reprinted with permission.

The circles of *Alphaville* are set in a straight line, because Lemmy Caution knows exactly who he is, what he is doing, where he is going; and in the end he triumphs over Alphaville, Capital of Pain, to win his love. But Pierrot, groping desperately to understand both life and himself, cannot find a path. "Suddenly I feel free," he exults, and while driving down a straight road, asserts his liberty by swinging the wheel to the right, only to land in the middle of an empty sea. Pierrot is trapped in circles within circles. Running away from his wife, he meets his former love, Marianne; but in escaping from his wife's efforts to better him socially and financially, he quarrels with Marianne over money and society;

and his affair with her ends in disaster, as it had done five years previously.

After the carefully ordered disorder of *Une Femme Mariée* and *Alphaville, Pierrot le Fou* looks like a return to the arbitrary insouciance of *Une Femme est une Femme,* "juxtaposing things which didn't necessarily go together, a film which was gay and sad at the same time." When Marianne first meets Pierrot and takes him back to her apartment, for instance, as he lies in bed next morning and she happily gets the breakfast, a casual shot reveals a corpse lying in the next room with scissors embedded in its neck. "I'll explain," says Marianne, and their flight to the Riviera looks like one of joy as much as panic; but her explanation, heard on the soundtrack as a series of inconclusive fragments, explains nothing, and Pierrot's questions, tortured by doubt, echo through the film like a refrain. Where *Une Femme est une Femme* picked out isolated moments (a shot of Karina crying followed instantly by one of her laughing), in *Pierrot le Fou* the ambivalence runs through the whole film as a cry of anguish for a world in flux where one can no longer *know.* "You won't ever leave me?" Pierrot asks anxiously, "You're sure?" "Quite sure," answers Marianne, gazing straight into the camera but obliged to drop her eyes before its searching gaze; and Pierrot is never sure.

Appearing briefly in the party scene at the beginning, Sam Fuller gives his definition of cinema: "Like a battleground. Love, hate, action, violence, death: in one word, emotion." *Pierrot le Fou* ranges freely over the battlefield – robbery with violence, pastoral idylls, murder by scissors, tender reconciliation – and its unity is purely emotional, radiating from Pierrot's attempt to understand and define his relationship with Marianne. He oscillates between happiness and unhappiness, and there are two main lines in his story, quite distinct though crisscrossed, subdivided, imperceptibly merging towards the final image of eternity. A line of romance in the flight through France, the Garden of Eden on the Riviera, the troubadour tales of Guynemer and the nephew of William of Orange told by Pierrot and Marianne to the tourists; and a line of despair in the world they escape from, the corpses which litter their path, the bitter parody of the war in Vietnam, the constant presence of betrayal.

The surface texture of the film is patterned by emotional associations. The aridity of Pierrot's relationship with his wife conjures up monochrome images at a society party where the guests chatter blandly in the jargon of television commercials; the absurdity of his marriage to a woman simply because she is rich ends in custard-pie comedy; his meeting with Marianne explodes in a burst of fireworks in the sky, and coloured lights flashing like meteors on the windscreen as he drives her away. The excitement of the flight to the Riviera brings thriller images of guns, cars, hold-ups, crashes; the tenderness of love brings verdant woods and a tranquil sea; and their quarrel evokes its parallel in a parody of the conflict in Vietnam. Wherever they go, Pierrot and Marianne are haunted by the aura of the world they live in, Vietnam echoing the atrocities of Algeria, through cinema, radio, newspaper headlines, conversation. Godard never forces the connections; all he does, in effect, is to point attention by reversing the perspective, making the background chorus of references seem foreground.

The theme of the film is stated in the opening quotation from Élie Faure on Velázquez ("After he was fifty, Velázquez no longer painted precise forms"), and later echoed by Pierrot himself: "Not to write about people's lives, but about life itself, just life. What lies between people . . . space, sound, colour . . ." *Pierrot le Fou* is an attempt to expand the momentary contradictions of *Une Femme est une Femme* through a whole film, and to examine the spaces, sounds and colours which lie in between being "gay and sad at the same time." On their itinerary through France, Pierrot suddenly scents the smell of death in the landscape, and a moment later decides that he feels just the opposite. "Life may be sad, but it's always wonderful." And even at the end, when he paints his face blue, wraps a roll of dynamite sticks round his head, and sets a match to it, his despair is uncertain, moving from the sad to the wonderful as he fumbles unavailingly to extinguish the match. In the course of the film, Pierrot swings from despair to ecstasy and back again. This is easy; what isn't so easy is to know where one leaves off and the other begins. The only certainty Pierrot ever finds is when both he and Marianne are dead; the camera pans slowly over a calm, glittering sea as their voices quietly murmur, "It has been found again . . . eternity."

It is a conception of pure romanticism – the story of *"le dernier couple romantique,"* as Godard himself puts it – and the most striking thing about the film, never obscured by its flighty pop art surface and characteristic jokes, is its lyrical tenderness, naked and unashamed and with none of the obliqueness with which it informs (always) the earlier films. Pierrot, like Gauguin in his flight to Tahiti, tries to find an untarnished world, and is doomed to failure. A spreading canker haunts the film with its signs: not only violence, indifference, brutality, war in Vietnam, torture in Algeria, death in Cuba, but also the enigmatic beauty of Marianne.

Pierrot looks on while Marianne, listening to a war communiqué from Vietnam, melts in tenderness (like Odile in *Bande à part,* Charlotte in *Une Femme Mariée)* for the 115 anonymous dead: "Each one of them is a human being, and we don't know who they are . . ." Yet this impulsive concern remains purely theoretical, for Marianne never discovers who Pierrot is, any more than he, despite all his efforts, discovers who she is. Like the sad tale of love misled by an obsessive song told by the man whom Pierrot meets on the pier, it is a tragedy of missed connections. Pierrot sees himself as a man about to drive over a cliff at a hundred miles an hour; Marianne sees herself as a girl in love with a man about to drive over a cliff at a hundred miles an hour; but meanwhile they are driving in opposite directions. "You speak to me with words, and I look at you with emotions."

The real key to this film is the search for lost time, Pierrot's murmured "Marianne . . . Renoir" over shots of Marianne herself, and a Renoir painting of a girl. His quest is for the romance of almost forgotten, nostalgic memory: the still air and pastel colours of a summer afternoon, green trees and shady lawns, girls with candid eyes and rosy cheeks. Innocent happiness, captured for ever in a painting by Renoir, whose ". . . nudes and his roses declared to the men of this century, already deep in their task of destruction, the stability of the eternal balance of Nature" (Jean Renoir's words). Nature, brilliantly captured in Raoul Coutard's photography, which makes one look in new astonishment at light and colour textures, dominates one half of the film in the sea, forests and beaches of the Midi, the green paradise which Pierrot and Marianne try to create with the fox and the parrot, the fields and the river they cross to get there. Equally present, dominating the other half of the film, is man's "task of destruction," in the arid cities and roads, punctuated red with lights, signs, cars, blood, until Marianne's red dress employed as an instrument of torture wrenches a despairing cry of protest from Pierrot: "I don't want to see the blood . . . I don't want to see the blood."

There's a progression: the desperate clutch at romance in *Bande à part;* the encroaching isolation in *Une Femme Mariée;* the anguish of *Alphaville.* And now *Pierrot le Fou* is a film of black despair clothed in all the colours of the rainbow as a last bastion against black despair. *"La vie est peut-être triste, mais elle est toujours belle."* Renoir's Nature is eternal, and hope, like Arthur's last vision of Odile in *Bande à part,* is the legendary Indian bird which never stops flying.

"EYE OF THE CYCLONE"

MICHEL CAEN

Cahiers du cinéma (from *Cahiers du cinéma in English,* Vol. 2. London: British Film Institute, 1966, 74), reprinted with permission.

If the brilliant beauty of *Pierrot le fou* makes an impression at first viewing, it remains no less true that this latest (soon next to the last) Godard discourages analysis on account of a dangerous obviousness that has been begged too often. The immediate temptation is to affirm defiantly the astonishing richness of the film, strike up a few aphorisms, and close the paragraph on a lyrical note that should answer possible contradictors ahead of time. So it is with a deplorable unconcern that the commentator would set out on a course of praise if only one question did not persist in disturbing his moral comfort: why does this new Godard appear to be situated in a new perspective in relation to the earliest works of this auteur? A second question – aimed at the difficulty of approach to the work by the roads of criticism – brings a rudimentary answer. If it is more difficult to write about *Pierrot le fou* than about *Les Carabiniers (The Riflemen)* or *Une femme est une femme (A Woman Is a Woman),* this is not because we are confronting a resumé – film or an anthology – as people have been only too willing to say. It is not a new facet that is offered us. Not even the synthesis of the earlier works, but more probably a new disclosure that compels us to reconsider the reference points we had been able to believe were definitely set.

In the multiple work of J.-L. Godard, bent on exploring new cinematographic regions, *Pierrot* occupies a place apart and marks perhaps the start of a new period, as *A bout de souffle (Breathless)* opened the chapter that would close on *Alphaville*. Work indeed multiple, still unclear to certain critics obstinately recognizing in it an incomprehensible uniformity, but whose most immediate aspect has been left in the shadow too often. Contrary to the opinion generally held even by those who praise his work, I have always thought that Godard addressed the sensibility of the viewer before addressing his intelligence. Only a deliberate desire to experiment presiding over the elaboration of each film has suc-ceeded in masking this essential quality until now. This time Godard refutes stylistic experimentation to make *Pierrot le fou* a continual questioning of the film itself. Without even the flimsi-est general line in advance, Godard seems subject to a necessity that belongs more to the film than to the auteur confronting this work as it elaborates itself day by day with a kind of passionate spontaneity that leads straight to the essential. As Sam Fuller defined it to Ferdinand-Belmondo, the cinema is a battle, and it is no longer a question of conjuring away its ups and downs from the public, but on the contrary of showing its slightest encoun-ters and reworkings to the point of making them the very essence of the work.

I don't mean that the technique is obvious here – as was the case for *The Collector* for example – but, on the contrary, that the film never preexists its shooting, and that every image reveals, as its watermark, the auteur's will to say everything and the rhythm of his own life. What then more natural, if the tempo of this action filming seems to be the heartbeat of a being bent on dis-covering, after a process that hesitates between Céline and Husserl, the tangible proofs of his existence? Before the film tilts toward this "controlled happening" that is the expression of life itself, the first sequences make up an entomological description of a congealed universe, a kind of air-conditioned nightmare that the auteur contemplates not without fear, witness the color filters that establish a necessary distance. To this spirit of scientific analysis (spectral decomposition) corresponds a new vision, polychromatic even to satiety, coincidental with Ferdinand's escape. But from the first chapter of this adventure, before the column of black smoke rises, or before he discovers the fatal signs in people's looks, Ferdinand knows that he is only a dead man on leave. He does not satisfy himself with learning this truth, he actually assimilates it to the point of making it his reason for living. That is why one must not smile (in spite of the ceaseless passages from the grotesque to the tragic) if he declares he wants to stop time because one morning, on the harbor, a slightly mad queen, the sunlight, some vibration of light and the presence of Marianne found again make him perceive more acutely than ordinarily the flow of life in his body. This new awareness will be accompanied immediately by another revelation superimposed on it, the impossibility of making two universes coincide entirely.

If Godard has willed to recompose an impression starting from its various elements, it is to the opposite process that Ferdinand gives himself, hoping by analysis to identify a phenomenon that escapes him since he himself is its center. Life is in him but its manifestations remain exterior to him. How to seize the central phenomenon? How can one film the eye of a cyclone?

Before this near-impossibility he assigned himself, Godard chooses to say everything at each image: anxiety, violence, the wavelength of solar radiation, death and the look of Marianne Renoir. The Godardian art of digression here reaches its culminating point, deliberately reducing the story to an "incoherent" web (incoherent in the customary meaning of the word) by a single-minded will to capture the event under a multitude of simultaneous lightings, an enterprise scarcely easier than photographing the other side of the nebula of Andromeda. Nothing astonishing, then, if this itinerary in the form of free fall offers us only episodic pulsations corresponding to the instants of calm. Clearly it is to paint life that Godard chooses to film the dead times, deliberately chopping the rare moments of action, conjuring them away, reducing them to the rhythm of the thought which does away with itself suddenly to concentrate itself into gesture, like an unforeseeable airpocket, to press a trigger, to plunge a blade into an absurd nape.

After having crossed a France changed for them to a tropical forest, Ferdinand and Marianne (or else it is Franz and Odile) recapture their own distances from which an artificial trajectory had removed them, the interval of one revolution. Marianne killed by his hand, all that remains for Ferdinand is to pursue this fall, suspended a moment, and now deliberate like that of Nicholas de Stael from the ramparts of Antibes. With a frenzy that we carefully civilized Occidentals will have difficulty understanding, mad Ferdinand – Ferdinand le Fou – dynamites himself, masked in blue, like the sea or that moon whose last inhabitant had run away to love Marianne, and wearing a tragically grotesque helmet of TNT. Perhaps all the film is contained in that last second when Ferdinand decides too late to extinguish the fuse. Perhaps Pierrot is this fraction of eternity before the explosion, these last visions that file past, they say, at 186,000 miles per second. Perhaps this hesitation sums up the entire work and gives new meaning to the sea, to this improvised ballet or to that electric blue set on flat white. In the end, to life, which, in the space of a deflagration, will have worn the horrible mask of a death in a day.

"BELMONDO PLAYS PIERROT TO ANNA KARINA"

RENATA ADLER

New York Times, 9 January 1969. Copyright © 1969 by The New York Times Co. Reprinted with permission.

"Pierrot le fou," which opened yesterday at the 72nd Street Theater, is one of the humblest and most gentle of Jean-Luc Godard's films. Shot in 1965, before the cracks in the young director's composure really opened up, the film has seams, murders, auto accidents, political harangues. The hero ultimately wraps his head in dynamite and blows himself to bits. But Pierrot is the "mon ami, Pierrot" from "Au Clair de la Lune" (a song that occurs uninsistently in the score), and a lot of the film's imagery is of the moon and gentle lunacy. It is in part a delicate, sentimental love story, a little on the order of Truffaut.

Jean-Paul Belmondo plays Pierrot, a writer whose girl calls him Pierrot, but whose real name, Ferdinand, is emblazoned on his sweatshirt. (He and the film have some of the sweet loser's ironies of Charlie Brown.) The girl is played by Anna Karina, Mr. Godard's first wife, and no film has ever been more loving in its treatment of a star. Miss Karina makes her particular case for life, clothes, dancing, fields, skies, love and a little violence, and the writer makes his abstract case for "Ambition, love, the movement of things, accidents – everything." They have an affair near the sea, with a fox and a parrot for company. They speak of Bernardin de St. Pierre's innocent "Paul et Virginie." They despair of each other.

They also have some "Breathless"-style adventures, with many references to Laurel and Hardy, "Johnny Guitar," Michel Simon, "Pepe le Moko" and other cinema presences that are exigently real to the imagination of Godard. The film requires a little patience as it goes its own erratic way. One long drive by night down a highway, with colored lights (the film, shot by Raoul Coutard, is in color) flashing incessantly across the hood and windshield is particularly trying in its affectation. So are the strainings to include a bit of Vietnam and politics. (When Godard is bad, he is terrible.) And the film generates a certain impatience in its oddly felt absence of any scene of sex.

But there is so much that is whimsical and beautiful: Pierrot, painting his face blue before he dies, and fumbling, at the last moment, for the fuse; Miss Karina, parodying musicals, unaffectedly singing (the music, from Beethoven to Duhamel, is a careful, thoughtout comment on the script); an incredible, isolated piece of highway overpass abandoned in a field; Mr. Belmondo putting mustard on an immense piece of cheese, during an authentic, cinéma vérité interview with a frowzy old eccentric who thinks she is queen of Lebanon; Jean-Pierre Léaud, appearing for one instant, looking baleful, on the screen; a kind of Brechtian bitter, fine misuse of American frames of reference, in the "Oh, Moon of Alabama" style; a superb comic turn, about love and refrains in the head, by the Belgian actor Raymond Devos.

The film is poetic, quiet, introverted, personal. The writer and Miss Karina have funny, despairing things to say to each other. There is no bravado in the part Belmondo plays this time, or any real violence in Miss Karina's. They are both charming and fed up, an idiom that sounds richer in French and that is applied in the film to everyone, including the man in the moon. One moving thing is that a director as proud and forceful, as annihilatingly positivist as Godard should make a film this tentative and forbearing about an artist and his girl in love.

"PIERROT LE FOU"

MARIE-CLAIRE ROPARS-WUILLEUMIER

Esprit 34 (1966).

With its record level of ticket sales, passion, and incomprehension, *Pierrot le fou* has brought Godard and his quarrel with the circle of cinephiles within the range of the general public. On the other hand, everything in the film derives from the earliest Godard: the anarchist adventure of *A bout de souffle,* the colors of *Le Mépris,* the parallel universe of *Bande à part* all converge here to compose life as a title sequence, a reconstructed puzzle assembled from letters.

"I put everything in my movies," Fellini has been saying from *8½* on; and this is indeed the ambition of a cinema that has for several years been trying to grasp hold of existence in order to comprehend it, that is to say, in order to apprehend it in its components. Whence the potential uncertainty in making judgments, and the variations in such judgments according to whatever order is revealed: either anything, anyhow, or a total necessity, a necessary totality. If in *8½* Fellini controls himself with creative order, in the totalitarian work that is *Pierrot le fou* all of Godard is achieved and possibly brought to an end. According to the encounter that may or may not take place between the sensibility of the spectator and the subjectivity of the work, each component, brought here to its maximum intensity, will seem to depend on either facility or harmony: an abuse of quotes or a productive breakdown of language; an appeal to the spectator's indulgence or a significant rupture of the narrative; a recourse to painting or an exploration of cinema. In fact, the balance so plainly achieved in the previous works is only realized here through instability; discord often succeeds fullness. For, as Godard says of *Pierrot,* true life does not speak, cannot recount itself, it rather possesses itself; as an image of that ideal life, the film tries to stop its course; but it cannot immobilize that flow without losing itself.

Rimbaud's poem, whispered into the void at the end – "It has been found again. What has? Eternity" – appeals, in order to complete itself, to another poem that is not named. Shouldn't one descend the "impassible rivers" [of *The Drunken Boat*] so that the sea might go "with the sun?" Once the bargemen are nailed "to painted poles," – red backgrounds, aggressive blues such as those against which the party guests stand out, naked at times – the voyage across France following its rivers finally leads to the sea, which a sudden movement of the camera will project into the sky. But eternity belongs only to death; in life it is boring. Another movement, which tears Pierrot from his island in spite of himself, will lead him from the sky to the coast, and in the end the sea will reign alone with death, in the final peaceful immobility of a long still shot.

The film has a unique structure: the problem is one of poetic continuity, says a fragment of Pierrot's diary (in fragments). But just as his contemplative dream is shown to be opposed to the active will of Marianne, so the cursory nature of cinema contradicts the poetic order chosen by the director.

Pierrot le fou represents a tentative limit to Godard's singular attempt to bring cinematic expression into the very essence of poetry. It belongs to poetry to compose, outside of time, the harmony of things and beings – words are reduced to images, images thrown toward words. Ferdinand's dream of possessing life as a poem is translated by Godard through a dream of a film that would exist only in space. Whence the novelty of his style: if all manner of languages keep entering into it as components, a new desire to arrest time is thereby manifested. To the reduction in montage there corresponds the insistent presence of long immobile shots where the movements of the characters who pass across the image and disappear from it constitute the very vibration of this invasive space: *Velázquez at the end of his life no longer painted precise forms, he painted what lay between the precise forms.* It is such an absence of definition that this pictorial technique attempts to evoke in the nature of its sequences as well as in the transitions to posters and paintings. It always amounts to framing beings against walls, or in a landscape, and to underlining in those same landscapes the dried lines of Cézanne's trees more than the evolving bloom of Renoir's flowers. For this poetic research tends to locate the structure rather than the effect of poetry; everything tends toward immobility, fixity, eternity: language ends in song, in dance, in silence.

If time sparkles, then in order to immobilize it definitively, one must break the thread of the story itself: Whereas ellipse and counterpoint, habitual for Godard, permit him to reduce a story to its interior line without destroying it completely, the constant doubling of the adventure and the adventurers in *Pierrot le fou* ends, on the contrary, by reflecting the narrative to the point of denying it: titles, chapters, sub-titles, narrative short-cuts, alternating commentaries by the characters whose off-screen voices at times stop and restart the same sentence, repetition of a line in two successive and different shots, the entire future of the action tends to be effaced by being stated, and the action itself ceases to exist even as it is being shown – "not blood, red," says Godard, because Ferdinand shouts: "I do not want to see blood." But in opposition to what happens in Brecht, or in Resnais, whom Brecht inspires, the point here is to contest rather than to contemplate the narrative; to evoke Verne, London, and Stevenson, to quote Faulkner and Céline, to show the Pieds-Nickelés or *ciné-romans* is to empty the action of its very substance at just the moment that it seems to materialize. The vision of the crazy Lebanese woman and the insane musician ruins the death of the heroes in advance; and the echoing of the essential themes completes this attempt to enclose time in similar images: a very long shot of a gray-green countryside follows the fire of the fake accident, just as the long shot of the gray-blue sea prolongs the explosion of Pierrot's suicide; it is with his face painted in the colors of the credits that he decides to die; and twice, at either end of the film, the arresting of time is associated with the same gesture.

But in this effort to abolish time, it is cinema's own rhythm that is in question, and the human or aesthetic materials, components of the meditation, stop being blurred by the narrative perspective that, in Godard's previous films, relieved them of their proper meanings in order to integrate them into a cinematic story. In a narrative that is rejected at each instant, words and beings are affirmed in ideas and sentiments; by refusing time and its rhythm, Godard gives literary weight to the literature that he uses; the monologues and conversations are far-reaching and explain all the more because it is impossible, given the way they are emphasized, not to hear them. The simplistic archetype of the treacherous and mysterious woman enters into dialogue with that of the confident and victimized man. This was already the schema of *A bout de souffle,* but there the narrative gave the characters a certain depth by staying with them. In *Pierrot le fou* Godard ignores psychology so completely that he falls prey to it: the relation between abstraction and the aesthetics of cartoons cuts both ways.

An insoluble contradiction thus appears between the absolute language of poetry and the narrative data of cinema, and it is indeed a contradiction that reflects very closely the opposition between Ferdinand and Marianne: Marianne lives in time while Ferdinand contemplates space. But by adopting only Ferdinand's point of view, that of poetry, Godard is condemned to being led by a narrative that he cannot control. After the dazzling departure of the Drunken Boat in the progressive acceleration of a bad dream, the fullness of the island gets confused by the spectator with the void of a time that stands still, reflecting on the elementary facts of the characters much more than on the complexity of their relations. And despite the beauty of the final return to the adventure story, such a recourse remains paralyzed by the fact that the adventurers are defined by that beauty.

Through its quest for a lost poetry, *Alphaville* reached the peak of poetic expression in film. But cinema can only suggest a search for poetry and, were it to attain it, it would disappear. Found even as it is lost, Eluard's poem shines in that film with several word-images torn by the cinema from sound and from the night. With *Pierrot le fou*, Godard, in attempting to maintain his grip on the poetic rhythm, risks losing cinema: dance, music, speech and painting, too often perceived for themselves, take on their own meaning instead of submitting themselves as material for the laws of another language. And far from being carried along by the rhythm of the story, the meaning of the film is instead born out of a certain failure of cinema. "True life is elsewhere." Godard's entire opus bears witness to this and more, in proportion as his language distances itself from the object it describes. But whereas the tragic grandeur of *Le Mépris* depended on a nostalgia that we recognize as belonging to tragedy, and *Alphaville*'s poetic beauty depended on declaring the death of poetry, *Pierrot le fou* produces a rupture: while trying for the first time to penetrate this *elsewhere*, inasmuch as it is unable to transmit it, the film confirms its impossibility.

(Translated by David Laatsch and David Wills)

Select Bibliography

Bellour, Raymond, and Mary Lea Bandy (eds.). *Jean-Luc Godard: Son + Image 1974–1991*. New York: Musuem of Modern Art, 1992.

Cahiers du cinéma (Spécial Godard – Trente ans depuis), November 1990.

Camera Obscura 8–10 (1980).

Cameron, Ian (ed.). *The Films of Jean-Luc Godard*. London: Studio Vista, 1969.

Cerisuelo, Marc. *Jean-Luc Godard*. Paris: Lherminier/Éditions des Quatre Vents, 1989.

Collet, Jean. *Jean-Luc Godard*. New York: Crown, 1970.

Dalle Vacche, Angela. *Cinema and Painting: How Art Is Used in Film*. Austin: University of Texas Press, 1996.

Deleuze, Gilles. *Cinema 2: The Time-Image*. Trans. Hugh Tomlinson and Robert Galeta. Minneapolis: University of Minnesota Press, 1989.

Dixon, Wheeler W. *The Films of Jean-Luc Godard*. Albany: State University of New York Press, 1997.

Douin, Jean-Luc. *Jean-Luc Godard*. Paris: Rivages, 1989.

Godard, Jean-Luc. *Godard on Godard*. Eds. Jean Narboni and Tom Milne. New York: Viking, 1972. This is the translation of the first edition of *Jean-Luc Godard par Jean-Luc Godard* (ed. Jean Narboni. Paris: Éditions Pierre Belfond, 1968), covering his work up to 1967.

Introduction à une véritable histoire du cinéma. Paris: Éditions Albatros, 1977.

Jean-Luc Godard par Jean-Luc Godard. Ed. Alain Bergala. Paris: Cahiers du Cinéma/Éditions de l'Étoile, 1985. Work up to 1967 is translated as *Godard on Godard*.

Lefevre, Raymond. *Jean-Luc Godard*. Paris: Édilig, 1983.

Lesage, Julia. *Jean-Luc Godard: A Guide to References and Resources*. Boston: G.K. Hall, 1979.

Loshitzky, Yosefa. *The Radical Faces of Godard and Bertolucci*. Detroit: Wayne State University Press, 1995.

MacCabe, Colin, Mick Eaton, and Laura Mulvey. *Godard: Images, Sounds, Politics.* Bloomington: Indiana University Press, 1980.

Monaco, James. *The New Wave: Truffaut, Godard, Chabrol, Rohmer, Rivette.* New York: Oxford University Press, 1976.

Pierrot le fou: A Film by Jean-Luc Godard. Trans. Peter Whitehead. London: Lorrimer Publishing, 1969.

Stam, Robert. *Reflexivity in Film: From* Don Quixote *to Jean-Luc Godard.* New York: Columbia University Press, 1992.

Williams, Alan. *Republic of Images: A History of French Filmmaking.* Cambridge, MA: Harvard University Press, 1992.

Index

Printed in the United States
By Bookmasters